Too many of our faith communities are not saf[e places for vulnera]ble people, and they are not safe spaces for the wounded. As a survivor, respected advocate, and prolific writer who loves Jesus and His bride, my dear friend Mary shares why and how to begin the journey of transforming the church into a community that protects the vulnerable and loves the wounded. This book is an invaluable resource that is so needed by today's church. Bravo, Mary!

Boz Tchividjian, attorney, law professor, founder and executive director of GRACE

DeMuth's gripping and transparent narrative of her own sexual abuse jolts the reader's emotions and ignites the Christian's mind. After reading this book, you'll be convinced that we too must never again be silent in the face of abuse.

Wade Burleson, author, historian, pastor

The church must do better when it comes to victims of abuse. This call comes not from a critic or a cynic but a lover of the church, an active member of a community of faith. Mary DeMuth's book does not merely point out the problems but also explains practical steps for the way forward. If the church follows Mary's advice, it will become a place of healing for the wounded and abused.

Glenn R. Kreider, professor of theological studies, Dallas Theological Seminary

Mary DeMuth has written a courageous book about sexual abuse. She rightly calls out churches for their complicity and complete failure to deal with the scourge of sexual violence. She also provides practical advice on what can be done. This book is necessary reading for anyone in Christian leadership.

Rev. Dr. Michael F. Bird, academic dean, Ridley College in Melbourne, Australia

Grounded in biblical truth, sociological research, and survivor stories, this comprehensive book will help readers wisely navigate the complex relationship between grace and truth, justice and forgiveness. Although I grieve that such a book is necessary, I thank God that Mary DeMuth has written it.

Jen Pollock Michel, author of *Surprised by Paradox*

Mary DeMuth's *We Too* is a timely gift to the church. With compassion and vulnerability, she opens a door into the heart, mind, and soul of sexual abuse survivors. With expertise and clarity, she instructs us in responding to sexual abuse and loving survivors. If every church leader and member took this book to heart, the church would be a safer and healthier place.

Eric Schumacher, pastor, author, and songwriter

In *We Too*, author Mary DeMuth is at her best. She speaks with the credibility of a survivor and as a well-informed expert. Her book helps readers assure that both their interpersonal relationships and faith communities are places of human flourishing. The church has been needing this resource.

Dr. Sandra Glahn, professor and coauthor of *Sexual Intimacy in Marriage*

I am grateful for Mary's life and her voice. We in the body of Christ need her. Her voice, along with many others, is the voice of our God calling his people into the light of truth and grace; to comfort the brokenhearted and release the captives. Read this book. Let it get inside you. Let it change you.

Diane Langberg, Ph.D., psychologist

Pastors, one of the most important and healing things we can do for survivors is listen. Mary has given us an excellent opportunity to begin listening in a form we are familiar with—reading a book. If we read biographies of other great saints (and we should), then let us read biographies of those who have faced one of the great tragedies of our day—sexual abuse—and maintained a great love for God, the gospel, and the church. Allow reading Mary's book to be a first step toward listening well to survivors in your church who need you to be the ears of Christ.

Brad Hambrick, pastor of counseling at The Summit Church (Durham, NC)

This book is a balm to the soul and a resource for the church at large. It is intelligently and discerningly written and initiates a healthy conversation over real and pertinent issues surrounding abuse within the church. #metoo

Vonda Dyer, CCO Minerva Consulting, worship leader, survivor, advocate

Mary DeMuth speaks a powerful and prophetic word that is timely and necessary. She courageously and vulnerably shares her experiences and shows her scars in a way that will embolden many others to do the same. *We Too* should be required reading for every pastor, church leader, and lay minister.

Rebecca Carrell, speaker, author of *Holy Jellybeans* and *Holy Hiking Boots*

In *We Too*, Mary DeMuth offers a prophetic and winsome call to the church to not repeat the mistakes of the past. She writes as someone who loves the church and is committed to its redemptive mission. We must do better as a church, and Mary helps point the way forward. A must read!

Aaron Graham, lead pastor, The District Church

Mary DeMuth's personal story, astute theological applications, and trauma awareness bring clarity to the passivity of the church toward countless men and women bearing the scars of sexual abuse. *We Too* is painfully necessary and yet filled with the hope of restoration for each person, family, and church affected by sexual abuse.

Brian Haynes, author and lead pastor, Bay Area Church (League City, Texas)

Instead of hearing voices of comfort and support, most abuse survivors experience silence, even from the church. Women deserve to be believed, and the church not only has a great opportunity, but a responsibility to respond.

Susan Seay, author, speaker, and host of the Mentor 4 Moms podcast

We Too is a remarkable and compelling book. Mary DeMuth prophetically calls the church to enter the silence and denial surrounding sexual abuse that has inflicted the body of Christ like a deadly virus. Victims of abuse, their family and friends, and those who shepherd the flock of God will find immense hope and clarity in how we are to find healing for individuals and a restoration of integrity for the church. There could not be a more perfect book for this time.

Dan B. Allender, Ph.D., author, founding president of the
Seattle School of Theology and Psychology

Mary invites everyone to the table with *We Too*—an honest, vulnerable, grounded, and biblical addition to the conversation of broken sexuality in the church and society. It's an authentic conversation about where we've been, the challenges we face today, and the hope of healing waiting in our tomorrow.

Antwuan Malone, pastor and executive director of ELEVATE YA

For too long the church has valued its reputation and the reputation of the accused over the safety and healing of the victim. DeMuth wisely shepherds the church toward a true biblical narrative demonstrating God's care and justice for the oppressed. A must read for every pastor, ministry leader, and Christian counselor.

Leslie Vernick, counselor, speaker, and bestselling author

Mary DeMuth brings wisdom to a difficult topic. She addresses challenges faced by all the groups affected by a single act of abuse, while offering insightful yet simple recommendations to ensure things are handled appropriately.

Ruth Thorogood, Evangelical Fellowship of Canada Partner

Carefully weaving the teachings of Scripture with her own story and the stories of others who have suffered sexual abuse, Mary DeMuth delivers a powerful wakeup call to the church she loves. Filled with biblical wisdom, factual evidence, and practical principles, *We Too* is an indispensable resource for anyone who cares about those who have been broken by sexual sin.

Bob Rognlien, author of *A Jesus-Shaped Life*

Mary DeMuth has a message that the church needs to hear. *We Too* is a transparent, thoughtful, raw, and honest account of a problem in the church that no one wants to talk about. But we must. *We Too* deserves to be widely read by women and men, leaders and laity. Don't miss it.

Kim Jones, director of engagement, My Refuge House

We Too is a prophetic call to embody Christ's healing, love, and justice for those oppressed by the powerful. It will take strength to walk humbly and courage to look at the mess. We can let go of the 30-second conversion narratives and instead sit with those bleeding in our pews. We can be the Good Samaritans again. Mary DeMuth boldly shows us the way.

Terri Fullerton, writer

I'm grateful to God that Mary DeMuth's journey, resilience, compassion, wisdom, and leadership have been shared in words clearly written with a deep love for the hurting and an undying hope for the church. *We Too* is a significant contribution to a church and society in need of healing, change, and a safer future.

Wade Mullen, director, Master of Divinity program,
Capital Seminary and Graduate School

WE TOO

MARY DEMUTH

HARVEST HOUSE PUBLISHERS
EUGENE, OREGON

Cover Art by Pixelworks Studios

Cover Design by Faceout Studio

> All the incidents described in this book are true. Where individuals may be identifiable, they have granted the author and the publisher the right to use their names, stories, and/or facts of their lives in all manners, including composite or altered representations. In all other cases, names, circumstances, descriptions, and details have been changed to render individuals unidentifiable.

We Too

Copyright © 2019 by Mary DeMuth
Published by Harvest House Publishers
Eugene, Oregon 97408
www.harvesthousepublishers.com

ISBN 978-0-7369-7918-4 (pbk)
ISBN 978-0-7369-7919-1 (eBook)

Library of Congress Cataloging-in-Publication Data

Names: DeMuth, Mary E., author.
Title: We too / Mary E. DeMuth.
Description: Eugene : Harvest House Publishers, 2019.
Identifiers: LCCN 2019004898 (print) | LCCN 2019011436 (ebook) | ISBN 9780736979191 (ebook) | ISBN 9780736979184 (pbk.)
Subjects: LCSH: Sexual abuse victims--Religious life. | Sex crimes--Religious aspects--Christianity. | Church work.
Classification: LCC BV4596.A25 (ebook) | LCC BV4596.A25 D46 2019 (print) | DDC 261.8/3272--dc23
LC record available at https://lccn.loc.gov/2019004898

Printed in the United States of America

19 20 21 22 23 24 25 26 27/ BP-SK / 10 9 8 7 6 5 4 3 2 1

*To all who have walked this perilous
journey of sexual brokenness and trauma,
I poured out this book as an offering of hope.
Oh, how I love you.*

*To Jimmy Hinton
who, along with his mother, Clara,
exemplifies the way the church can redemptively
support the sexually abused
and represent what it means to be agents
of justice in an unjust world.
Oh, how I thank you.*

CONTENTS

AS YOU READ THIS BOOK:

May the Holy Spirit cast down destructive mindsets and
strongholds—strongholds controlling people's lives
within the body of Christ.
May *We Too* be a prophetic call of release
for both survivors and the church.
May this initiate an Isaiah 61 ministry to set captives free—
those sinned against and those who sin.

May blind eyes see your truth,
deaf ears hear your Word,
mute tongues release your Word,
and walls of deception and bondage be smashed.

May your people rise up with a renewed sense of identity.
May they know who they are.[1]

FOREWORD

FROM J.D. GREEAR

In light of the growing awareness of how poorly abuse has been handled by almost every institution in our culture, where should the church begin to address the crisis among us?

By listening.

Listening does at least two things. First, listening restores voice and dignity to the survivor. During abuse, voice is ignored. Or marginalized. Or silenced outright. After abuse, a sense of voice is often lost. A church that does not listen communicates that what a survivor experienced doesn't matter to God or God's people.

Second, listening removes ignorance from the church and church leaders. We need to understand as much as survivors need to be heard. Ignorance on our part makes us ill-equipped to be ambassadors of Christ. Survivors of abuse are in every one of our congregations. Potential victims are, too. How tragic if we neglect to protect them because our ears were found closed?

Mary DeMuth has given a great gift to the church. Not only has she courageously written her story, but she has also represented the stories of countless other survivors. She knows their stories because she has listened to their stories. And now she steps forward as their advocate.

Pastors, this is an opportunity for us to listen. Mary DeMuth is a survivor of sexual abuse who loves God and loves his church. It is *because* of this love that she has shared her story. And her example can encourage many others to do the same.

Reading this book will make us uncomfortable. There is no pleasant way to write about the experience of abuse, no matter how redemptively we write. But ignoring painful truths, or listening to them only half-heartedly, has paved the road to where we are now. Survivors ask something of us that perpetrators do not. Trauma specialist, Judith Herman, articulates this succinctly:

> "It is very tempting to take the side of the perpetrator. All the perpetrator asks is that the bystander do nothing. He appeals to the universal desire to see, hear, and speak no evil. The victim, on the contrary, asks the bystander to share the burden of pain. The victim demands action, engagement, and remembering."[1]

Of all people, Christians ought to be aware that abusers can infiltrate even the best of institutions. Jesus told us that after his departure "shepherds," who cared nothing for the flock, only wanting to use and abuse it, would come in his name (John 10:12, cf. Ezekiel 34:2). Sexual abuse is not a problem limited to one belief system, one creed, or one organizational structure. It's not a Roman Catholic problem. It's not a Hollywood problem. It's our problem.

The question before the church is whether we will have eyes to see, ears to hear, and courage to speak. Will we be ambassadors of the Great High Priest who is willing to sympathetically and personally engage every form of human suffering? We serve a God who gave his life to protect the vulnerable. How dare we turn a blind eye and deaf ear to the vulnerable in our midst?

This book is not only a warning. It is an opportunity. An opportunity to live out the gospel we so passionately proclaim. And it starts with listening.

There is a remarkable power in simply listening. The damage done by silence and isolation is only matched by the healing that is possible through hearing with compassion. Hearing is not the whole of healing, but it is a simple and powerful first step. As DeMuth puts it, "I healed because people dared listen to my story and pray for me."

As M. Scott Peck famously said, "To listen to someone is to love them."

How do we become ministry leaders who are caring for people rather than responding to an issue? Let me offer several suggestions as you read this book:

- Read this book in a posture of listening. Seek to understand, not to argue. This book raises hard realities. But the church needs them. And thankfully, DeMuth says them in love. So pray for the strength to avoid becoming defensive.

- Buy a second copy of this book and give it to a survivor you know. Use it to prompt a conversation about how their experience was similar to and different from DeMuth's. Honor them with the experience of being heard.

- Invite this friend to share with you the ups and downs of their personal challenges of living in the aftermath of abuse. Ask them to share with you their experience when future tragedies and scandals are revealed in the church (as they inevitably will be).

A final word: If abuse is close to you—especially if it is part of your story—you may need to read this book slowly. Remember that our God is the Good Shepherd who walks through the valley of the shadow of death with his sheep (Psalm 23:4). He doesn't stand on the other side and urge you to hurry your way out of it. He climbs down into the valley and walks with you through it.

Mary: Thank you for the church-loving, gospel-centered, vulnerable honesty of this timely and necessary book. Thank you for exercising your voice in calling us to listen as the beginning of love.

On my birthday, a joint investigative piece by the *Houston Chronicle* and the *San Antonio Express News* highlighted sexual abuse within the largest protestant denomination in the United States, the Southern Baptist Convention (SBC).[1] The ripple effects of this investigation will no doubt be felt even as you read this book. The article highlights the ease of sexual predators to prey on many people, freely moving from congregation to new church without hindrance. Couple this with shocking evidence that the Catholic Church in Germany destroyed records of sexual abuse allegations or simply did not bother to record abuse, and you see how deep and wide this scourge is—following the common narrative of disclose, demean the victim, cover up the crime, and allow the predator space to reoffend.

I grieve the pervasiveness of cover up, though I will not let its cancer silence me. My grief has morphed into holy urgency.

Why? Simply this. I believe God is cleansing his house, the church. I picture Jesus, hands clenched around a whip of cords, expelling those who have acted as bad shepherds. He epitomizes the good shepherd in John 10, and what does that shepherd do? "The good shepherd sacrifices his life for the sheep" (11). Yet so many leaders who name the name of Christ have, instead, acted this way: "A hired hand will run when he sees a wolf coming. He will abandon the sheep because they don't belong to him and he isn't their shepherd. And so the wolf attacks them and scatters the flock. The hired hand runs away *because he's working only for the money and doesn't really care about the sheep*" (John 10:11-13, emphasis mine). Sexual predators are wolves. But so often we have seen wolves protected, sheep slaughtered, and money within the structure of churches preserved. This should not be.

In the opening chapter of *We Too*, I write about the Good Shepherd and the Good Samaritan, exegeting the wisdom of both metaphors as it relates to our current crisis. But there is one thing I recently recognized in the latter story. Not only did the priest and Levite walk by the attacked victim, they also never alerted authorities. They couldn't be inconvenienced to act justly, even if that meant doing relatively nothing, except to simply tell someone else.[2] This is the crisis we face—a crisis of lackadaisical inertia. My heart in writing this book is not to merely highlight our current plight, but to inspire truth telling, boots-on-the-ground advocacy, and a conspiracy of active empathy. We can do better. We *must* do better.

I am not without hope, though. In the aftermath of these scandals, my church, an SBC megachurch, sent the following email:

Many of you have read recent news releases about sexual predators who over the last few decades have attempted to use churches as a place to act out their evil crimes. Please know that Lake Pointe remains committed to being a safe and secure place for all our children.

In addition to using video surveillance and requiring background checks for those who work with our children, we will continue to enforce strict policies about the care of children, including immediately notifying authorities of any and all reports of abuse. We also will support and contribute to any collaborative communication effort to keep offenders from moving from church to church undetected, exposing future victims to risk.

We are also deeply committed to provide a healing community of faith that expresses the gentle love of Jesus for the thousands of men and women of all ages who have been victims of sexual abuse at any time in their lives.[3]

The letter concludes by directing people to counseling services.

While the world casts stones at places of worship for the mishandling of abuse cases, there are congregations around the world quietly providing solace and help to victims, reporting perpetrators to the proper authorities, welcoming independent investigations, and communicating honestly with their members about failures in leadership. This brings me hope. There are good shepherds among us who beautifully represent Jesus, the Good Shepherd. There are good Samaritans within our gatherings who dare to see the hurting, bandage their wounds, provide resources, and love well. It is my sincere hope that *We Too* will play a small role in ushering in a new era of transparency, kindness, redemption, and the undecorated rightness of doing good.

Your story matters,
MARY DEMUTH

FIRST

THE EXAM ROOM, THE BACK DOOR, AND THE DANCE FLOOR

I am sorry on behalf of all men for all the awful things
that have ever happened to you. I'm desperately sorry.

MALCOLM

THE EXAM ROOM

Only my husband, Patrick, knows this story (and now, you). This is the first time I've written it down, ink to screen, stark naked on the page like I stood when it happened—when *he* happened. Pregnancy (my first) wreaked havoc on my body, delivering a healthy baby girl *and* hemorrhoids. New to this town, I had yet to find a general practice doctor, so I called around to locate one quickly, making sure he or she carried my insurance. Knowing the ailment's posterior locale, I already carried humiliation's sting. Giving birth hadn't been an angel's-chorus event either—it was a stalled, lengthy labor where an overzealous anesthesiologist pushed enough painkiller to knock out a gorilla, leading me into a deep panic, certain I wasn't breathing.

"You're talking, Mary," Patrick had assured me that day. "That means you're breathing."

I pulled in a breath now, then shivered in the sterile hospital gown, socks still on my always-cold feet. I looked at my pile of clothes on the chair, wishing my underwear still graced me.

And the exam room? Four beige walls that pressed in on me while my heart thrummed panic. The doctor entered. No nurse stood beside him, just this man with a smile pasted on a placid face. I'd never experienced this, *ahem*, issue before, and my twentysomething naïveté must have advertised itself like flashing neon. At that time, I hadn't yet shared widely about my experience of sexual abuse at five years old—a deeply painful story that reared its fanged head when I delivered my baby girl, yelping and vulnerable in a world that still traumatized me. What if teenage boys targeted her as they did me? I could barely bring those thoughts to the light of day because if I did, I'd vomit.

I sat on the very edge of the exam table, arms closed around myself like skin-and-bone armor while the room pressed in like a Star Wars garbage chute. "I need you to stand up," the doctor said.

I obeyed.

I always obeyed.

He turned me away from him, strong fingers clenching my shoulders, then paused behind me. I inhaled his mothball breath. I didn't know rectal examinations could be done discreetly, as I balled myself on a table, a nurse or other attendee holding my hand, witnessing the exam, giving me a shred of dignity. I didn't know that a doctor standing creepily behind me, breathing heavily, holding my shoulders in locked place, was not a typical practice.

He parted the back of the gown and lingered longer than a pregnant pause. He told me to bend forward, backside naked. I've blanked out most of this memory, but I am pretty sure he didn't wear gloves. All I know is that I was told to stand in that position for a very long time, and the exam hurt like crazy. There were moments when he wasn't probing, which meant he spent what felt like several claustrophobic minutes standing back and examining me from behind as I bent. If I close my eyes while I write this, I can see the dingy room, smell the fear, take note of the doctor's greasy hair and leering eyes.

I considered myself astute to the ways of sexual predators. After repeated rapes at five, I'd become a running fool, sprinting away from many boys and men trying to trap, coerce, and molest me. That first yearlong abuse marked me indelibly, my personhood emitting some sort of predator beacon, drawing them toward me. They chased. I ran.

I thought I could spot a predator easily. But this one's sleight of hand and command of the room dizzied my thinking.

Back in college, I dared to tell my story out loud. Letting it out into open air ushered in the beginning of health. I "completely" healed, or at least that's what I told myself. I didn't understand the nature of complex trauma, that getting well is never simple. It's not a one-and-done phenomenon. Healing is a years-long saga of stops and starts and stutters. When I decreed that I'd been healed, this shaky belief stunted further growth. Because of the monstrous ugliness of what I endured throughout my childhood, I had to believe the myth that knowing Jesus made everything perfect. Because if I believed that down to my cold toes, I would no longer have to travel back to the salted air of Alki Beach in Seattle, to the hemlock-haunted park where the brambles and thorns bit my pink skin, and those two boys stole everything from me: dignity, a carefree heart, trust, and innocence.

It took me a while to tell Patrick what the doctor did to me, how I flustered my clothing back on, triple-thumbed, while I buttoned my shirt cockeyed, how my heart fluttered fear, beating faster and faster still. And it shakes my heart to write it down today. Because I realize again that although there are amazing people in this world, there are also predators—men and women intent on stealing life from innocent survivors. This is cold, documented fact. Predators permeate every strata of society. My first abusers were Boy Scouts. This man? A doctor. They infiltrate trustworthy structures like organizations, sports, and, yes, even the church.

THE BACK DOOR

The evangelical church has not done a good job of loving those broken by stories of sexual assault, discrimination, and harassment. We have forsaken the admonition of Isaiah 58:6: "No, this is the kind of fasting I want: Free those who are wrongly imprisoned; lighten the burden of those who work for you. Let the oppressed go free, and remove the chains that bind people." Instead, we blame the enslaved. We have run the extra mile to validate the protests of the indignant "caught" predator with the result that we're too far away to hear the quiet cries of their victims.

There is a holy reckoning unfolding before us in the church—a white-hot exposure of those who have stolen, killed, and destroyed others. This is a necessary corrective for those who have either blamed and shamed survivors or created elaborate facades for cover-ups. Sadly, the secular media has shown more compassion for sexual abuse casualties than those who populate the pews and pulpits of this nation. I write this after the grand jury investigations of most of the dioceses in Pennsylvania have been made public. These investigations revealed torturous stories of abuse accompanied by systematic, almost methodical cover-up for years on end.

The 2015 movie *Spotlight* may have had evangelicals tsk-tsking their superiority, but we suffer from the same issues. Youth pastors are arrested nearly weekly for inappropriate sexting, sexual assault, and solicitation. Mega pastors have lost reputation, integrity, and membership in the aftermath of sexual harassment and cover-up. Like the Catholic Church, we've been guilty of shuffling predators from church to church, giving them carte blanche to offend again. This is a watershed moment for the church, and how we deal with it while the world watches *matters*. We can no longer retreat into the "holy" cloisters of our own making, wearing our Sunday best while predatory people commit crimes against the innocent.

Boz Tchividjian, one of Billy Graham's grandsons and the founder of GRACE (Godly Response to Abuse in Christian Environments), witnessed this kind of dichotomy when prosecuting child sexual abuse cases. "The few cases that I had that involved a faith community, I saw the faith community respond to it in a terrible way," he said. "More often than not, if the pastor or member of the church came to court to speak on behalf of somebody, it was on behalf of the perpetrator, and not the victim."[1] He recounts seeing a smattering of the victim's family members sitting on one side of the courtroom, while nearly the entire church sat behind the perpetrator on the other side, offering support.

My friend Jimmy Hinton faced something so egregious, it is painful for me to write the story. When his sister, Alex Howlett, disclosed that their father sexually molested her, Jimmy had a decision to make. Keep the secret so his father, who had been the longstanding pastor of the church Jimmy now pastored, would have an intact reputation, or bring this abuse to light. He, along with his mother, turned his father in to the authorities soon after Alex's disclosure. The investigation uncovered multiple little-girl survivors. It led to his father's arrest, a guilty plea, and conviction. He is now serving a 30- to 60-year prison sentence for his crimes. Jimmy shared the following insight on his podcast. Alex's disclosure and the police's uncovering of his father's serial predation, he said, "completely shattered everything I knew about a protective God." He continues:

> There was a period of time when I almost flat out hated God for, in my mind, sitting idly by, while my dad acted as a monster and hurt all these innocent kids. So I kept asking that question. *Where were you, God? Where were you when all this was going on?* And finally…I had this overwhelming sign that came to my brain. [God said] "You're asking the wrong question. The question was not where was God when all this was happening. The question is, where were God's people?" And that was such a pivotal moment for me because we are the hands and feet of Jesus, and we have the opportunity to prevent this stuff from happening, and we're not doing it.[2]

Jimmy's words sober me. They should sober us all. *Where were God's people?* Grievously, some of them were preying on others.

A serial offender who wrote several Christian books, coached countless Christian writers, and pioneered one of the premier Christian college writing departments in the USA stepped down after many accusations surfaced about inappropriate behavior toward women and students. His retort? He blamed the #MeToo movement. "Now this is coming out 14 years later, with this whole 'Me Too' kind of thing, and everyone is piling on the bandwagon."[3] Perhaps people are piling on the bandwagon because the bandwagon is headed in the direction of justice and truth. Perhaps this is yet another indication that our society, where millions of people live in the aftermath of sexual abuse's devastation, has finally gotten fed up with this grievous behavior. This is *our* issue. And we are tasked with doing something redemptive about it. Yet it's an unspoken and seldom articulated crisis within the evangelical church. Despite living in the waning years of the attractional church model, we have succeeded in wooing many through our front doors with relevant teaching; powerful, concert-like worship; and a myriad of family-friendly programs—with charismatic, celebrity pastors at the helm. Yet our painful, untold story is about the crowd of broken people flooding through our back doors, many of them women who have been victimized.

They are leaving because they are not being shepherded. They are leaving because their brokenness is treated with contempt, inconvenience, or dismissal. They are leaving because we have preferred protecting our reputations over listening to the cries of those who have been violated. They are leaving because they are not heard, valued, or welcomed. They are leaving because they feel utterly alone in their stories and because so few abuse stories are even hinted at on Sunday mornings.

While we long to see the church grow deeper through discipleship and wider through evangelism, instead we are experiencing a shameful exodus of the very people who could offer the world the kind of authentic, raw hope the next generation craves and needs. We are losing our clarion voice because of our nearsighted fear of how messy caring for them can be. And yet, they are the ones Jesus pursued when he walked this earth. And, I would argue, they are the very people who can teach us to love the world for which Jesus died. The abused are our tutors, but we've expelled them.

The Good Samaritan story found in Luke 10:25-37 is as relevant today as it was when Jesus uttered it. Jesus shared it in response to a religious leader asking, "Who is my neighbor?"—a seemingly benign question. He details the misfortune of "a man" who is attacked, robbed, and left to die in a ditch. Two religious leaders pass by the man, indifferent to his plight, refusing to tend to the needs of the injured party. Only a Samaritan outcast notices the man's plight, inconveniencing himself to tend to wounds, provides for the survivor's care, and exemplifies what a neighbor actually does in a broken world.

Today there are men, women, and children who have been robbed, coerced, shamed, belittled, beaten, marginalized, and sexually assaulted who are sitting quietly in padded chairs, feeling unseen while some leaders pass by on the other side. Survivors are often afraid to speak up, for fear of marginalization or dismissal.

And lately, we can see why. Leaders within the evangelical community have scoffed at survivors daring to tell their stories. They have minimized abuse, using rhetoric that morphs it from a criminal felony to a minor infraction—a sin issue to confront, not a crime to report. Some congregations have stood to applaud sexual predators. They have covered up abuse within their well-protected and powerful ranks and then embarked on shame campaigns against anyone who speaks out. They have even revictimized the survivor—*something so grievous Jesus didn't even place that reaction in the Good Samaritan narrative.* At least the religious people walked on by on the other side of the road. But today, we are guilty of grabbing the nearly unconscious innocent and retraumatizing him or her with judgment-laced platitudes or downright callous harshness.

The reason there continues to be an exodus from our churches is that the Good Samaritans of the world outside our churches have provided far more help and empathy than the church has. *This should not be.* The church, by its very nature, is mandated to be a haven for the broken, a community where needs are mutually met (see Acts 2:42-47). But we are living again in a time where Ezekiel's prophetic words ring true:

> You have not taken care of the weak. You have not tended the sick or bound up the injured. You have not gone looking for those who have wandered away and are lost. Instead, you have ruled them with harshness and cruelty. So my sheep have been scattered without a shepherd, and they are easy prey for any wild animal. They have wandered through all the mountains and all the hills, across the face of the earth, yet no one has gone to search for them (Ezekiel 34:4-6).

We need to start searching.

We perplex over why people stream out the back doors of our churches. It's because we have not properly made disciples—the heartbeat and longing of the church, the great heartbeat of the gospel. We love evangelism. Our mission boards espouse and revere the Great Commission. To disciple another is to walk alongside, to hear, to teach, to reproduce our faith in Jesus, infusing his love into the life of another. Discipleship is about relationship, connection, conversation, prayer, and powerful empathy. But if we dismiss the hurting, the broken, and the abused, we cease being the disciple-making church, and we instead become citadels of unreality and privilege. In short, we shirk the joyful responsibility it is to truly disciple everyday people.

Ever notice how broken and outcast people flocked to Jesus, the Good Shepherd? Hurting people did this because the Good Shepherd exemplified the Good Samaritan, and that kind of love is powerful. Jesus was irresistible to the marginalized. They couldn't help but long to be in his presence because he listened, dignified, and healed them. He didn't treat them as religious projects or numbers on a baptism tally sheet. No, they were people, flesh and blood like the marginalized Samaritan woman. Unfortunately, we have lost our irresistibility, replacing it with the idol of stability and status quo. We find ourselves protecting what *is* rather than redemptively imagining what could be, what *should* be.

We Christians love a good turnaround story, don't we? We love testimonies of people moving from darkness to light. But if we continually push away those who are broken and beaten by the darkness, how will we ever see the audacity of light-infused redemption? The redemption of God shines brightest on the darkest backgrounds, and yet we have deemed those priceless works of art (Paul calls them *poiēmata*, creations) as worthless. We have walked conveniently on the other side of the road, forgetting that Jesus wears the upsetting disguise of the marginalized, those bleeding in the ditch. Those who have experienced the hell of darkness, then the healing of Jesus—they have the best stories.

I am haunted by these words of Jesus in Matthew 25:41-45:

Then the King will turn to those on the left and say, "Away with you, you cursed ones, into the eternal fire prepared for the devil and his demons. For I was hungry, and you didn't feed me. I was thirsty, and you didn't give me a drink. I was a stranger, and you didn't invite me into your home. I was naked, and you didn't give me clothing. I was sick and in prison, and you didn't visit me." Then they will reply, "Lord, when did we ever see you hungry or thirsty or a stranger or naked or sick or in prison, and not help you?" And he will answer, "I tell you the truth, when you refused to help the least of these my brothers and sisters, you were refusing to help me."

It's time to heed these difficult words of Jesus, because we find Jesus in the face of the domestic abuse survivor. He wears the pain of the sexually assaulted. He is the one left naked and bleeding and vulnerable—it's how he's depicted on the cross. Undressed in my doctor's office, I understood a smidgen of what Jesus must have felt.

The pathway forward is not easy, because it involves truth—the kind of truth that cuts through darkness and exposes the hidden motivations of all people's hearts. It involves admitting systemic failure, religious pride, and, in some cases, denominational refusal to see what is right in front of them. It will mean specific rather than generic apologies, genuine face-to-the-ground repentance, and a commitment to change backed by purposeful action. It will mean a radical recommitment to the Great Commission, making disciples of all people. It will mean a return to shepherding, to modeling Good Samaritan behavior from our pulpits to our pews.

I write this book not as an indictment against the church, but as one who dares to have prophetic imagination for what it can and should be. I love the church. And because I love it and have not left it, I have a stake in its glory. If we address these painful, unseemly elephants in the room, we will experience revival, reformation, and a holy relevancy.

People are longing for apology, humility, and gentleness. They're so deeply wounded by the protective nature of the institutional church that they've stopped going altogether. We need survivor's voices, their unique perspective. And they need our shepherding, understanding, and kindhearted prayer. If we stand together, the Great Commission flourishes. Separated and fragmented, we lose our witness.

Atticus Finch is famous for these words in *To Kill a Mockingbird*: "You never really understand a person until you consider things from his point of view—until you climb into his skin and walk around in it."[4] In order to overcome this systemic loss of confidence by our most vulnerable members, we must put on the sandals of the Good Samaritan and the Good Shepherd, cross over to the places where people are broken, bind up their wounds, and empower them to heal. A church that does this will change the landscape of the kingdom of God, one broken heart at a time.

A TALE OF TWO CATS

While in Yvoire, a medieval French town on the banks of Lake Geneva, I spotted a cream-colored, friendly looking cat perched in an ancient windowsill. He did not approach me, but I walked toward him, saying, "Here kitty, kitty," as if he would understand English. (He was a French cat, after all.) He flicked his tail. I reached out to pet him, but his response was to hiss, bite, and scratch me. As I walked away, I chided myself for approaching him. He must have known many, many tourists in the past, and no doubt there were some who acted malevolently toward him. He was rightly cautious.

A few days later, after teaching a course on writing in the outskirts of Geneva, Switzerland, I took a leisurely walk after a long week of pouring myself out. I sensed God telling me to pay attention—to listen, to look, to fully embrace the countryside. I approached an old home, then spied a calico cat in the field beyond it. I bent low to the ground, and called out, "Here kitty, kitty" again by instinct. Though the cat was at least a city block away from me, she stood, then trotted toward me through the field. Now at my feet, she allowed me to pet her, scratch her neck, and pick her up—all while purring. When I put her down, she circled in and out of my legs. I thought, *She must have people in her life who love her. She trusts me.* As I type this, her fur remains on my black pant legs.

As I completed my walk, I realized I represented the worst and best of the church in my European cat encounters. To the cat that had negative encounters with humans, I represented trauma. Trust, in light of that pain, became impossible. To the cat that had positive encounters with humans, I represented kindness and safety. Trust was her natural instinct.

I fear that the church has so traumatized survivors by unfeeling, caustic, or disbelieving responses that it's no wonder they're not only uninterested in our services, but their default is to hiss, claw, and bite. My hope in writing this book is to slowly change the dynamic of trust by encouraging the church to become a consistent place full of kindness and safety for those who have been exploited. My holy longing is that we can create such a haven for the sexually broken that they'll begin to respond like the second cat, able to be loved, feel joy, and revel in relationship. I believe the shift beckons—and I've experienced it in South Africa.

THE DANCE FLOOR

I've been shattered in as many pieces as I'd been taken advantage of, harmed, dismissed, and pushed away. I've been accused of not wanting to heal (though I've pursued healing in so many ways). When I tell my story, some recoil from it, no doubt wishing I would just be quiet and not speak of the past. Sexual abuse and trauma are painful, and the shame of those experiences thrives in darkness. One sad truth I've learned over the years is that the church doesn't like messy. The church prefers a neat, victorious story, tied up with a cliché bow, full of manufactured piety and pasted-on "joy." Seldom is there room for questions, wrestling, anguish, grief, or bewilderment because that somehow connotes that those who were harmed are not "walking in faith."

But one man noticed me, my pain, my shattering. He changed everything for me. I met Malcolm in Cape Town, South Africa, at Cape Town 2010, the Lausanne Congress for World Evangelization. I went as one of the representatives of the United States, a humbling, surprising privilege. I volunteered to be a table host, where I led discussions with five other believers throughout the conference. We would dialogue about what we heard from the stage—stories of redemption, persecution, and God's beautiful kingdom. We hailed from many nations: Iraq, South Africa, Nigeria, the UK, Zimbabwe, and we each had a chance to share our stories within a circle of trust. I told my story too.

On the last day of the conference, Malcolm, who hailed from Johannesburg, beckoned me. While people began taking down the props of the venue, he held my gaze. He faced me, gently touched my shoulders—in the opposite posture of the doctor who had stripped me of dignity. Instead of me stretching toward my toes, Malcolm, a man in his sixties, sank to his knees before me, tears releasing from his ocean-blue eyes. "Mary," he said, his South African accent lilting. "I need to tell you something."

I knew then that something significant stretched out before me. It's one of those times I sensed the Lord say, *You need to listen. Be in this moment. Take it all in.* Malcolm struggled to keep his composure. "I apologize," he said. "I am sorry on behalf of all men for all the awful things that have ever happened to you. I'm desperately sorry."

I didn't know what to say. His words stunned me to silence. No one had ever, ever attempted to apologize for such a thing, to take on the mantle of all that sin against me—except Jesus. "Will you forgive me? Will you forgive us?"

I wept a *yes* his way. He stood. We hugged. And I walked away changed. Instead of excuses or dismissals, instead of tolerating always-broken me, instead of wishing away my story, instead of blaming me for my pain, Malcolm said the words that flattened my container of grief, transforming it into a dance floor, where freedom and yet another layer of healing surfaced.

That's my hope for this book. We may begin the journey imprisoned. But dare to adventure alongside me, hear the echoes of the Scriptures we love so much, step into the shoes of those who have suffered, hold the hand of the One who bore the weight of every single sexual sin, and venture out onto the dance floor. Freedom awaits.

PART ONE

UNDERSTANDING OUR ROOTS

CHAPTER ONE

RAPE: THE BIBLICAL CONUNDRUM

"No, my brother!" she cried. "Don't be foolish! Don't do this to me! Such wicked things aren't done in Israel. Where could I go in my shame? And you would be called one of the greatest fools in Israel. Please, just speak to the king about it, and he will let you marry me." But Amnon wouldn't listen to her, and since he was stronger than she was, he raped her.

2 SAMUEL 13:12–14

I f you want to see everything that hell can vomit our way, read the Bible. It's part narrative, part poetry, part prophetic warnings, part songs, and part laments with the same sin-tainted DNA that bedrocks our stories. The fall of humankind is a reality. And immediately after the fall, shame entered the human experience, followed by violence, separation, and depravity. And with all that, sexual predation entered the world. Essentially, the serpent's lie fueled the frenzy. If we believe we are gods, then we can violate anyone we deem lesser than us. As God has granted us free will, we have exercised it for our violent hedonism—at the expense of the other.

Before we continue exploring this painful narrative, let's pause to build a quick foundation. What is sexual abuse, exactly? The American Psychological Association defines it this way:

> Sexual abuse is unwanted sexual activity, with perpetrators using force, making threats or taking advantage of victims not able to give consent. Most victims and perpetrators

know each other. Immediate reactions to sexual abuse include shock, fear or disbelief. Long-term symptoms include anxiety, fear or post-traumatic stress disorder.[1]

Sexual abuse is an act of power and control over another, often using verbal threats (and sometimes physical) to keep the abused quiet. The spectrum ranges from unwanted sexual innuendo...to forced rape; from creating a hostile, sexually charged workplace...to sexual slavery; from an unwanted hand placed on the unsuspecting person's leg...to forcing someone to watch porn; from forcing a child to become a surrogate spouse...to a teacher flirting with a student; from forcing a committed partner to "consent"...to the use of a date-rape drug.[2] While some sexual abuse is categorized as shock-and-awe (when a jogger is attacked, then raped by a stranger), most often the survivors know their abusers, and the abusers are powerfully adept at grooming their prey, action by subtle action—so much so that victims feel a strange affinity to the one abusing them. Abusers are not strangers lurking in the shadows—they are often charming, "good" citizens who fit well into society—it's why they get away with their behavior over the long haul. While there may not be violence involved as we often narrowly define it, any form of sexual control over another is a violent act.

God feels very strongly about violence, so much so that excessive violence (and no doubt, this included sexual violence) ushered in the flood—a swift act of judgment and condemnation. "Now God saw that the earth had become corrupt and was filled with violence. God observed all this corruption in the world, for everyone on earth was corrupt. So God said to Noah, 'I have decided to destroy all living creatures, for they have filled the earth with violence. Yes, I will wipe them all out along with the earth!'" (Genesis 6:11-13). The Hebrew word for "corrupt," *shachath*, has several connotations, but includes ravaging, bringing to ruin, destruction, depravity, laying waste, spoiling, and devastating—all words that aptly describe the aftermath of sexual violence. The word "violence," *chamas*, connotes malice, physical violence, harsh treatment, unjust gain, cruelty, damaging, oppression, and injustice—again words that many sexual abuse survivors relate to.

While entire books have been written about sexual violence in Scripture, my hope for this chapter is to give you an overview of abuse within its pages—not pulling back from the raw narrative, but presenting it frankly. We've been trained to think benevolently in looking at heroes of the faith, seldom questioning the starkness of each story. We reason away King David's multiple wives and concubines, painting over his sin with the broad stroke of "he was a man after God's heart." It's important we give ourselves permission to ask questions of the text. David T. Lamb reminds us of this:

> Paul said all of Scripture—including what we might consider the R-rated stories of the Old Testament—is God-breathed and can train us in righteousness (2 Tim. 3:16-17). It's not that we skip over such stories, but that we tend to use euphemisms when telling them. We don't pay close attention to the details, and as a result miss what the biblical authors intended to communicate. Stories not just of prostitutes, adulterers, and fornicators, but also of sexual predators and human traffickers.[3]

In Genesis 12, we see Abraham "essentially trafficking" his wife, Sarah, by telling her to say she's Abraham's sister. Lamb asserts:

> God called Abraham to be a blessing to all families of the earth, including his own. But he does the opposite here. He was more concerned about his own safety than his wife's wellbeing and dignity. (And Abraham repeats this cowardly, selfish act in Genesis 20.) Sarah must have felt betrayed, and Pharaoh suffered because of Abraham's deception: God sent plagues to punish Pharaoh for taking Sarah as his wife (Gen. 12:17). The only one "blessed" in this scenario is Abraham. He essentially trafficked his wife and profited richly, and it didn't take long for sexual exploitation to creep up again in his family.[4]

Later we see his same pattern repeated by Abraham's son Isaac with his wife, Rebekah, in Genesis 26:1-33.

SODOM AND GOMORRAH

In Genesis 19, we see a disturbing picture of Sodom and Gomorrah, where Lot offers his daughters in lieu of the visiting angels to townspeople raging to rape. After the family's narrow escape, sans Lot's salt-pillared wife, his two daughters got their father drunk and had incestuous sex with him on two subsequent nights.

> The next morning the older daughter said to her younger sister, "I had sex with our father last night. Let's get him drunk with wine again tonight, and you go in and have sex with him. That way we will preserve our family line through our father." So that night they got him drunk with wine again, and the younger daughter went in and had intercourse with him. As before, he was unaware of her lying down or getting up again. As a result, both of Lot's daughters became pregnant by their own father. When the older daughter gave birth to a son, she named him Moab. He became the ancestor of the nation now known as the Moabites. When the younger daughter gave birth to a son, she named him Ben-ammi. He became the ancestor of the nation now known as the Ammonites (Genesis 19:34-38).

These daughters violated their father. Were their actions echoes of their own trauma? Was that violation their form of revenge? Did they overhear their father offering them like cattle to the angry townspeople? The names of the nations that sprang from these unholy unions give us clues—Moabites and Ammonites were godless nations that opposed the people of Israel. The biblical narrative is otherwise silent on the outcome of this deviant act, but the inference cannot be discounted. There are consequences, possibly generational, when someone overpowers another (this time via alcohol) and takes sexual advantage of them.

DINAH

Later, in Genesis 34, we see the rape of Dinah, stark on the page:

One day Dinah, the daughter of Jacob and Leah, went to visit some of the young women who lived in the area. But when the local prince, Shechem son of Hamor the Hivite, saw Dinah, he seized her and raped her. But then he fell in love with her, and he tried to win her affection with tender words. He said to his father, Hamor, "Get me this young girl. I want to marry her" (Genesis 34:1-4).

Here we begin to see the Jekyll and Hyde nature of a sexual predator who stalks, grabs, rapes, then tries to appease with words of marriage. The fallout of this interaction ends with vigilante justice by Dinah's brothers. They convince the entire tribe to be circumcised through deceptive words, then slaughter the men of the tribe, retrieving a disgraced and traumatized Dinah.

Jacob (Dinah's father) has a peculiar response, more concerned for his status and welfare than the safety and reputation of his daughter. We see this pattern play out in today's church, where churches circle the wagons, trying to control the narrative while the survivor fades into the background.

Afterward Jacob said to Simeon and Levi, "You have ruined me! You've made me stink among all the people of this land—among all the Canaanites and Perizzites. We are so few that they will join forces and crush us. I will be ruined, and my entire household will be wiped out!" (34:30).

Their attempt at justice for Dinah's sake now made it hard for Jacob to live peacefully amid pagan cultures—something that should have already been difficult. The brothers, indignant, retorted, "But why should we let him treat our sister like a prostitute?" (34:31).

Whereas Jacob had been relatively passive in response to Dinah's rape, the brothers had not. Whereas Jacob had agreed to intermarry with Shechem's people (a clear violation of God's instructions), his sons deceived and then destroyed them. It's also important to note that God is not mentioned in this entire passage. No one asks God for intervention or justice. No one prays. No one offers palliative help to Dinah—she is almost viewed as property that's been stolen rather than a human being who's been violated. In light of this, we have to remember that just because a story exists within the Bible's pages doesn't mean the story is a mandate of how to behave. We must not confuse a descriptive scene with a prescriptive command.

MOSES

In Numbers 31, we read another difficult story during the conquest of the Midianites. The Israelite warriors have conquered the land, but left some alive. With anger, Moses asks:

> "Why have you let all the women live?" he demanded. "These are the very ones who followed Balaam's advice and caused the people of Israel to rebel against the LORD at Mount Peor. They are the ones who caused the plague to strike the LORD's people. So kill all the boys and all the women who have had intercourse with a man. Only the young girls who are virgins may live; you may keep them for yourselves" (verses 15-18).

Whether or not "keep them for yourselves" is an indication of future violation and rape as a spoil of war is unclear in the text. But in this narrative, again, we don't see Moses consulting the Lord as to what he should do. We are left in the conundrum of where God is in the case of abuse of power and sexual violence.

Moses seeks to clarify God's heart about sexual violation in two legal passages from Deuteronomy. He writes:

> But if the man meets the engaged woman out in the country, and he rapes her, then only the man must die. Do nothing to the young woman; she has committed no crime worthy of death. She is as innocent as a murder victim. Since the man raped her out in the country, it must be assumed that she screamed, but there was no one to rescue her. Suppose a man has intercourse with a young woman who is a virgin but is not engaged to be married. If they

are discovered, he must pay her father fifty pieces of silver. Then he must marry the young woman because he violated her, and he may never divorce her as long as he lives (22:25-29).

These passages are difficult to read with a Western, postmodern mindset, but to understand the gist of them, we have to contextualize the narrative. The Hebrew words for sexual violation vary, as you can see in the English translation—"rapes" versus "has intercourse." The first word for "rape" is *hāzaq*, which connotes forcible intercourse. The second word, *tāpas*, means to "capture by seduction." It's the same word used when Potiphar's wife tried to seduce Joseph. Katie McCoy elaborates:

> Further, *tāpas* does not appear in either of [the] biblical stories describing sexual assault that were written after the Law. When later biblical authors depicted a rape, they used the *hāzaq* (which appeared vv. 25-27) rather than *tāpas*. We can reasonably conclude that the biblical narrators (and again, the Holy Spirit) knew the difference in meaning between *hāzaq* and *tāpas* within the context of sexual violence, and they used these verbs with their meanings in mind.[5]

THE CONCUBINE

Echoes of Lot's encounter in Sodom and Gomorrah can be found in Judges 19—a passage that begins ominously: "Now in those days Israel had no king" (19:1). Later, we see this frightening narrative:

> While they were enjoying themselves, a crowd of troublemakers from the town surrounded the house. They began beating at the door and shouting to the old man, "Bring out the man who is staying with you so we can have sex with him." The old man stepped outside to talk to them. "No, my brothers, don't do such an evil thing. For this man is a guest in my house, and such a thing would be shameful. Here, take my virgin daughter and this man's concubine. I

will bring them out to you, and you can abuse them and do whatever you like. But don't do such a shameful thing to this man." But they wouldn't listen to him. So the Levite took hold of his concubine and pushed her out the door. The men of the town abused her all night, taking turns raping her until morning. Finally, at dawn they let her go. At daybreak the woman returned to the house where her husband was staying. She collapsed at the door of the house and lay there until it was light. When her husband opened the door to leave, there lay his concubine with her hands on the threshold. He said, "Get up! Let's go!" But there was no answer. So he put her body on his donkey and took her home. When he got home, he took a knife and cut his concubine's body into twelve pieces. Then he sent one piece to each tribe throughout all the territory of Israel. Everyone who saw it said, "Such a horrible crime has not been committed in all the time since Israel left Egypt. Think about it! What are we going to do? Who's going to speak up?" (verses 22-30).

The question at the end of this narrative haunts me: *Who's going to speak up?* There isn't a better, more clarion call for the church today. Yet this horrible crime—awful as it is—is being duplicated worldwide today in a dastardly festival of pornography-fueled lust. Men, women, boys, and girls are being trafficked for the sake of the sexual appetites of others. We must weep. We must grieve. We must speak up.

I find it compelling that not many years later, King Saul committed a similar act of butchery, but to cows:

> He took two oxen and cut them into pieces and sent the messengers to carry them throughout Israel with this message: "This is what will happen to the oxen of anyone who refuses to follow Saul and Samuel into battle!" And the Lord made the people afraid of Saul's anger, and all of them came out together as one (1 Samuel 11:7).

This further reinforces the way that this ancient society viewed women—as chattel to be herded, managed, and disposed of.

BATHSHEBA

Though scholars differ on King David's interaction with Bathsheba, you see a clear power differential—one of the essential elements of sexual exploitation—in the narrative in 2 Samuel 11. Sexual assault is an abuse of that power. Some say that Bathsheba meant to entice David, that their sexual encounter was consensual, even romantic. But consider the reality: David was king; she was his subject. He ruled the land—a warrior of strength and power. Even if she did "consent," the power differential always prevailed. Lamb puts it this way:

> Why blame her? She could have been fully clothed and [bathing] using just a bowl. The text doesn't say she was naked. And the text doesn't say she knew she was being watched. Finally, women generally didn't say no to men—not in ancient societies like theirs. And subjects certainly didn't say no to kings. While the first half of the story is ambiguous about the extent of her guilt, the second half is pretty clear about who is to blame. The text and the characters point the finger at David. God blames David.[6]

Nowhere in the narrative is Bathsheba blamed. Nathan the prophet, sent from God, doesn't address her, shame her, or tell her she shouldn't have been bathing at that time. He certainly didn't ask what she was wearing. All blame is leveled at the king, who loses their firstborn son, then suffers irreparable damage the remainder of his reign. The consequences of his behavior echo in the interchange between the prophet and the king when Nathan confronted David with a story of a poor man with a lamb:

> "One day a guest arrived at the home of the rich man. But instead of killing an animal from his own flock or herd, he took the poor man's lamb and killed it and prepared it for his guest." David was furious. "As surely as the LORD lives," he vowed, "any man who would do such a thing deserves to die! He must repay four lambs to the poor man for the one he stole and for having no pity" (2 Samuel 12:4-6).

David recognized the unjust treatment of the man and his beloved lamb, calling it stealing and worthy of death. Certainly, those who have walked through sexual abuse, rape, harassment, or predation would call the encounter death-like—death to dreams, innocence, and fearlessness. It is the violent theft of identity, volition, and personhood.

TAMAR

Abraham's trafficking of Sarah had generational consequences, as evidenced by Isaac's treatment of Rebekah. Similarly, David's sin moved down his lineage to his son Amnon, who falls in "love" with his sister Tamar in 2 Samuel 13. His adviser, Jonadab, advises him to pretend to be ill, and when his half sister serves him, he could then take her, which he did, though she protests: "'No, my brother!' she said to him. 'Don't force me! Such a thing should not be done in Israel! Don't do this wicked thing'" (verse 12 NIV). She pleads with him to no avail. "But he refused to listen to her, and since he was stronger than she, he raped her" (verse 14 NIV). This is clearly rape. He tricked; he forced; she said no; he overpowered and then raped. He then despises her and asks his servant to lock her out of his room. Tamar's response is poignant and comprehensible to anyone who has experienced such violation:

> She was wearing an ornate robe, for this was the kind of garment the virgin daughters of the king wore. Tamar put ashes on her head and tore the ornate robe she was wearing. She put her hands on her head and went away, weeping aloud as she went. Her brother Absalom said to her, "Has that Amnon, your brother, been with you? Be quiet for now, my sister; he is your brother. Don't take this thing to heart." And Tamar lived in her brother Absalom's house, a desolate woman (verses 18-20).

Later, Absalom avenges Tamar's rape, but his response in the moment after the violation serves to remind us of modern-day responses.

Be quiet.

He is your brother (pastor, teacher, boyfriend, husband).

Don't take this thing to heart.

Clearly, Tamar withered under this callous, nonempathetic advice. She lived out her years desolate. Once beautiful, a girl with promise, the king's daughter, she became a sequestered exile who lived without hope. Sadly, when we tell sexual abuse survivors to be quiet, then to submit to silence for the sake of the reputation of the one who abused, all while encouraging them not to take things to heart, the raped wither as well. Shame flourishes in silence. And in the case of Tamar, it steals her future. No longer a virgin, she will not be marriageable. The narrative, thankfully, reveals the abject desperation of Tamar and the obvious, sinful predation of her half brother—it does not sugarcoat it. But that honesty doesn't take away the very real consequences of the rapist's actions. It's important to note that in all three of these cases of rape—Dinah, Bathsheba, and Tamar—war broke out after their defiling, followed by justice.

HAGAR

Perhaps it's important to back up again in the biblical narrative to Genesis 16 and look at the life of the Egyptian Hagar, the concubine who bore Abraham's first son, Ishmael. Used, abused, and fleeing (her name means "flight"[7]), she has two powerful encounters with God, who dares to hear and see her. On her first runaway attempt, she runs into the angel of the Lord, who asks, "Hagar, Sarai's servant, where have you come from, and where are you going?" (16:8). It's a complex question that reveals God's compassion and empathy to someone who had been exploited. God wants to know her story, and he is concerned for her future. (If churches today would simply ask those two questions, we'd see a revival of healing in our midst—to listen and dignify a story is freeing, and to dream about the future alongside someone who has suffered trauma is redemptive.) The angel tells her the name of her upcoming child: Ishmael—it means "God hears." Then she becomes the first person in Scripture to give God a name. "Thereafter, Hagar used another name to refer to the LORD, who had spoken to her. She said, 'You are the God who sees me.' She also said, 'Have I truly seen the One who sees me?'" (16:13). God hears. God sees. When no one else does, God intervenes.

Later, in Genesis 21, when Hagar flees again, this time she finds herself and her son starving—utterly alone and in quiet desperation. The one who names God falls into despair. She walked away from her son, who was dying of malnutrition, because she couldn't bring herself to watch him die. In that moment, God heard and saw, asked a question, then gave a command with a promise attached: "But God heard the boy crying, and the angel of God called to Hagar from heaven, 'Hagar, what's wrong? Do not be afraid! God has heard the boy crying as he lies there. Go to him and comfort him, for I will make a great nation from his descendants'" (21:17-18).

What if our churches responded to survivors of sexual abuse in a like manner? What if we dared to ask the question, "What's wrong?" while truly being interested in the person's response? What if we empathetically came alongside and gently encouraged someone away from fear and toward faith by believing them, helping them get safe, and pursuing appropriate justice? What if we, like the angel of God to Hagar, proclaimed prophetically a belief in the beauty of future possibilities?

The heart of God hearkens toward those who have been sexually exploited. Consider the myriad passages about the quartet of the vulnerable (widows, orphans, the poor, and aliens) throughout the biblical narrative—God is concerned for the downtrodden, and he punishes those who oppress the least of these.

We think of Hagar as a blip on the Pentateuchal radar—an interesting aside. But consider this: How would we know she had radical encounters with God unless she said something to those in power? How did Moses know her story? She fled. But she also must have spoken about what she suffered and encountered. That's the power of story. Her testimony serves as an encouragement to all survivors of betrayal, exploitation, and marginalization. God heard her. God saw her. He hears those who mourn. He sees those who suffer under the weight of other people's exploitation.

GENEALOGIES

In the next chapter, we'll look at how Jesus approached those who have been violated. As we do, it's important to notice the genealogies pointing back to several women who also found themselves in vulnerable positions.

The Matthew 1 (NIV) genealogy mentions five women: "Judah the father of Perez and Zerah, whose mother was Tamar" (verse 3); "Salmon the father of Boaz, whose mother was Rahab, Boaz the father of Obed, whose mother was Ruth" (verse 5). "David was the father of Solomon, whose mother had been Uriah's wife" (verse 6). "And Jacob the father of Joseph, the husband of Mary, and Mary was the mother of Jesus who is called the Messiah" (verse 16). The first woman, Tamar, prostituted herself with her father-in-law in order to preserve her husband's lineage. The second was Rahab, also a prostitute, who risked her life to protect the nation of Israel as it attacked Jericho. The third woman mentioned, Ruth, who was also a non-Jewish outsider like Rahab, appealed to Boaz as her kinsman redeemer, thus restoring her mother-in-law Naomi's fortune and genealogy. Fourth was Bathsheba, whom Matthew does not name. He emphasizes the fact that she had first been Uriah's wife—highlighting David's egregious sin against her and God. The fifth is Mary, the virgin who must have endured awkward looks and conversations about her pregnant status.

All of these women had difficult stories. Many were oppressed and harmed. And yet, they live and breathe in the genealogy of Jesus Christ. In a patriarchal culture, the mention of women in the genealogy of the Son of God is utterly astounding. It shows that no matter what we've walked through, even if that journey involved sexual exploitation, our lives still matter in the kingdom, and, I would argue, our voices matter even more.

CHAPTER TWO

THE REVOLUTIONARY RESPONDER: JESUS

Yes, just as you can identify a tree by its fruit,
so you can identify people by their actions.

MATTHEW 7:20

While it's dangerous to split the Testaments—viewing God as wrathful in the Old Testament and affectionate in the New—the practice is understandable. We resolve the seeming discrepancy by understanding the entire narrative of the story arc of God—a God who was not taken by surprise when Adam and Eve learned of their nakedness in the garden after the serpent's sly deception. God had a plan to redeem mankind—a plan that originated with a people, Israel, who were to be a light for the world, a beacon of hope, and a pathway to knowing the God who created us all. But a thorough reading of the Old Testament reminds us just how far the nation of Israel fell, preferring idolatry and sin to serving their Maker, let alone sharing with the vulnerable about the redemptive nature of God. In the intertestamental period, the silence of God is deafening, but he shouts the next phase of his plan with the birth of Jesus Christ—the God-man, perfectly sinless, perfectly human, who came to bear the weight of humanity's sins.

Before we look at Jesus and his interaction with the relationally broken, we must come to grips with his empathy for those who suffer. The Scripture reminds us that he was tempted in all possible ways, yet did not sin (see Hebrews 4:15). He encountered every nuance of pain and temptation the devil could throw his way in the wilderness, and he bore it all while in a starved and thirsty state. And when the Romans stripped him of everything he wore at the very end of his life—everything but a crudely woven crown of thorns—Jesus experienced the humility of public nakedness. Stripped. Bare. Exposed. Mocked. Utterly unclothed. While Scripture doesn't record that Jesus experienced sexual assault, we can be assured that he must have felt degraded and exposed—something every sexual abuse survivor has felt at one time or another. Our beautiful, empathetic Savior understands what it's like to live in this violent, sexually charged world. He knows betrayal and physical pain.

SILENT SUFFERER?

Jesus was both silent and loquacious when he faced this torture and mocking. He stood silent in the Synoptic Gospels (Matthew, Mark, and Luke), spotlighting his connectedness to the suffering servant mentioned in Isaiah 53:7: "He was oppressed and treated harshly, yet he never said a word. He was led like a lamb to the slaughter. And as a sheep is silent before the shearers, he did not open his mouth." Yet in the Gospel of John, we see his response to the high priest: "Everyone knows what I teach. I have preached regularly in the synagogues and the Temple, where the people gather. I have not spoken in secret. Why are you asking me this question? Ask those who heard me. They know what I said" (John 18:20-21). Next, we see Jesus interacting with Pilate as well.

Why bring up this distinction? Because some, horrifically, have used Jesus's silence in the face of suffering as a prescription for abuse survivors, telling them that it is godly to keep abuse silent. The latter interactions in John undermine this argument, and if anything, Jesus's words, "I have not spoken in secret," refute this silencing takeaway.

If anything, we see Jesus wooing people to speak, to tell their stories. And as he walked this earth, he saved his most significant interactions for those who were broken. In the woman at the well discourse, he holds his longest theological discussion recorded in the New Testament—with a despised Samaritan outcast, a woman who most likely experienced sexual marginalization. In my coauthored book *The Day I Met Jesus*, I wrote her story in narrative form based on much research. Consider the possibility that she could have been barren, then dismissed by her husbands:

> In all, five Samaritan husbands had me. Four husbands used my body, then dismissed me. Only one loved me, but my happiness died with him. I shook my fist at the Almighty, daring Him to take my life and be over with it. Why should I remain here on this earth? Without a child, I had no legacy, no hope, no reason to live. There existed none to carry on my traits or my lineage or my sorry story...I have heard it said that a barren woman must always send herself to get water because she has no children to bear the weight of labor. Halfway to the well, I wondered again (was it the millionth time?), why am I here in Samaria? What is the reason God placed me on this sullen earth? Does He create people simply to be used and abused? Has His favor shone only on the Jews? Only on the strong? Only on men? Only on women whose wombs produced babies? He certainly did not shine upon me, even as the sun relentlessly accosted me on my long, lonely walk.[1]

In John 4:27-30, we see the end of the story unfold:

> Just then his disciples came back. They were shocked to find him talking to a woman, but none of them had the nerve to ask, "What do you want with her?" or "Why are you talking to her?" The woman left her water jar beside the well and ran back to the village, telling everyone, "Come and see a man who told me everything I ever did! Could he possibly be the Messiah?" So the people came streaming from the village to see him.

This broken woman, cast aside by her village, her people, and the disciples as unworthy to be dignified with conversation, becomes a passionate missionary. There is no shame in her declaration ("See a man who told me everything I ever did!"); instead, freedom laces her words. When world-weary people interact with Jesus, they leave the conversation utterly freed and alive.

AN EXPLOITED WOMAN

When Jesus interacts with the woman caught in adultery in John 8:1-11, there is no man similarly caught. According to Leviticus 20:10, both parties must be punished: "If a man commits adultery with his neighbor's wife, both the man and the woman who have committed adultery must be put to death." Where is the man? Because of his conspicuous absence, many scholars believe the woman was used by the Pharisees as a theological trap for Jesus. She may have even been raped.

Jesus turns the tables on the Pharisees' desire for blood and instead forces them to look at their own propensity for sin. From oldest to youngest, the crowd (including the Pharisees) walks away, all aware of their bent toward sin. And when Jesus tells the woman to go in peace and sin no more, it's not necessarily a rebuke of her ostensible adulterous sin, but a statement for all of us: When we encounter Jesus, we are changed, and our new lives reflect that transformation. It's important to note that Jesus saw the woman's distress and desperate situation and rescued her from it. He alone was qualified to stone her, but instead of a stone, he offered grace.

In a world system where survivor-blaming has reached epidemic heights, Jesus's emancipation of the woman caught in adultery is beautifully instructive. Never did he demand, "What were you wearing?" or "What did you do to get yourself into this predicament?" He simply rescued her from an impossible situation.

SUFFERING SERVANT

Jesus embodied his own words: "Whoever wants to be a leader among you must be your servant, and whoever wants to be first among you must become your slave. For even the Son of Man came not to be served but to serve others and to give his life as a ransom for many" (Matthew 20:26-28). While abuse in any form involves an abuse of power and clutching at control over others, we see Jesus demonstrate the opposite. He laid down his power, willingly giving it up to serve those in need. Although he holds the universe together (see Colossians 1:17), he allowed for others to harm him, giving up rightful control. Philippians 2:5-8 beautifully illustrates this laying down of power, known as *kenosis*, in this passage:

> You must have the same attitude that Christ Jesus had. Though he was God, he did not think of equality with God as something to cling to. Instead, he gave up his divine privileges; he took the humble position of a slave and was born as a human being. When he appeared in human form, he humbled himself in obedience to God and died a criminal's death on a cross.

Think about the audacity of *kenōsis* for a moment. In a world where men and women claw their way to power and prominence, Jesus, who already had it, let it gloriously go. As God the Son, he could have demanded allegiance. He could have destroyed any perceived enemy. He could have used his deity to create a life of ease and privilege, but instead he walked the dusty streets of Palestine, without a place to lay his head other than a stone pillow. He spent many sleepless nights interceding for humanity, and he, the Bread of Life, often went without food. He became the downtrodden. He became the broken. He became the marginalized. He became the abused. He did this for us and for the glory of his Father, who tasked him with saving the world. He faced off with Satan, our great enemy, in the wilderness, receiving every possible spiritual, mental, and physical attack. He did all this because of love.

EMPOWERING THE DISENFRANCHISED

Jesus loved women—a marginalized demographic in his day (and in ours in much of the world as well). He listened to them, asked questions, empowered them. He allowed for their voices to be heard.

He had Rabbi-disciple conversations—the type typically reserved for men—with Mary of Bethany. Women were the first reporters of the resurrection. A popular T-shirt reminds us: "Jesus protected women, empowered women, honored women publicly, released the voice of women, confided in women, was funded by women, celebrated women by name, learned from women, respected women, and spoke of women as examples to follow. Our turn."

But his acts of empowering didn't stop with half of humanity. Take a walk through the Gospels and you'll see Jesus interacting with those who had no hope in the Roman "kingdom"—demoniacs, crippled people, the woman who bled for years, lepers, immigrants, humble fishermen, prostitutes (who were most likely trafficked or economically compelled to do what they did), grieving parents, the woman bent over double (see Luke 13:10-17), thieves, the poor, the sick, and the marginalized. Yet these outcasts became the insiders to another kingdom—a kingdom where the first are last and the least are most. Jesus knew that those who were unfit for a world system (Rome's) were actually closer to the kingdom of God because they knew their need and lack. Those who are broken by this world understand their need for a Savior, and they are more apt to cling to Jesus than those who are puffed up and self-important.

This is why the apostle Paul later recounts a conversation he had with Jesus, who told him, "My grace is all you need. My power works best in weakness" (2 Corinthians 12:9). This is the secret of Jesus, the audacious hope for the sexually abused. Our weakness, the very thing we despise and think disqualifies us from life and happiness in this life, is actually the very thing that makes us fit for the kingdom—through Jesus.

STRANGE KINGDOM DICHOTOMY

Jesus speaks of this strange dichotomy in the Sermon on the Mount. Look at the paradoxes:

> God blesses those who are poor and realize their need for him,
>   for the Kingdom of Heaven is theirs.

God blesses those who mourn,
> for they will be comforted.
God blesses those who are humble,
> for they will inherit the whole earth.
God blesses those who hunger and thirst for justice,
> for they will be satisfied.
God blesses those who are merciful,
> for they will be shown mercy.
God blesses those whose hearts are pure,
> for they will see God.
God blesses those who work for peace,
> for they will be called the children of God.
God blesses those who are persecuted for doing right,
> for the Kingdom of Heaven is theirs.

God blesses you when people mock you and persecute you and lie about you and say all sorts of evil things against you because you are my followers. Be happy about it! Be very glad! For a great reward awaits you in heaven. And remember, the ancient prophets were persecuted in the same way (Matthew 5:3-12).

Now reread these verses as a sexual abuse survivor. Those who are stolen from in this heinous way are certainly poor in power, yet Jesus says he grants kingdom privileges to them.

The aftermath of sexual abuse is a heavy mantle of grief. I've spent years grieving the multiple rapes I experienced at five, and in the midst of that grief, I've experienced the comfort of Jesus. (But please hear me: I'm not saying Jesus makes everything shiny and happy. Sexual assault has lasting, traumatic effects. Therapy, prayer, medication, and good relationships help as well.) To be humble is to understand your place in this world, and if you've been traumatized, you have already experienced a crushing humbling. While a sense of safety may have been stolen from you, Jesus promises an eternal inheritance that cannot be shifted or stolen. The abuse survivor has a keen sense of justice woven into their being, longing for the wrong to be made right, for the perpetrator to face justice, for those harmed to be healed. Jesus promises satisfaction. Those who have allowed their abuse to make them empathetic and merciful will themselves experience divine mercy. Though an understanding of purity is hard for a survivor to grasp after violation, we are promised a clean heart through Jesus's life, death, and resurrection—not to mention the ever-present gift of the Holy Spirit. And who doesn't long for peace in the aftermath of sexual exploitation? The father heart of God beckons our broken ones. We, who are belittled and battered, are now called his children.

The latter part of the Sermon on the Mount shouts hope to those who have suffered. We speak up and tell our stories not just for ourselves, but for the sake of others. We bring light to the darkness in order to expose the plots of the evil one who longs to steal, kill, and destroy humanity. And what better way than to enslave them through sexual exploitation? By bringing this issue into the light, we are partaking in important spiritual warfare, but, in doing so, we will experience secondary trauma. Though the church should be the safest place on earth for abuse survivors, sadly it is not, and often it is our own fellow church members who mock us, belittle us, attack our character—all for the sake of keeping things quiet. But Jesus promises another nugget of joy here. We have a great reward in heaven, and by shedding light in the dark, we align ourselves with prophets who experienced the same shaming.

THE ACTUAL BODY OF JESUS

We complicate things when it comes to church. We forget that the church is meant to be the actual body of Christ. We are the hands and feet that represent Jesus Christ to a broken, sin-entrenched world. We are his ambassadors of healing love, blessedly counterintuitive to the world's system that grabs at power and control. Sexual abuse is fueled by these twin sins. And when the abuse happens within the walls of the church, we often see a clash of kingdoms. Instead of acting as Jesus would toward an abuse survivor, we revert to the kingdom of power and control, preferring reputation management to actually doing what is right: protecting and providing healing for the wounded and justice for the one who harmed.

RESTORATIVE JUSTICE

After Jesus dined with Zacchaeus the tax collector, he declared, "Salvation has come to this home today, for this man has shown himself to be a true son of Abraham" (Luke 19:9). What happened? This known Roman-sanctioned thief blatantly harmed and took advantage of his fellow countrymen, extorting more money than the tax laws required. Jesus spies the short-in-stature man in a sycamore tree and invites himself over for dinner. In the midst of the meal, this notorious man encounters the love of Jesus. In a moment that must have been both horrifying and freeing, Zacchaeus realizes that his life has been solely about exploitation. He declares, "I will give half my wealth to the poor, Lord, and if I have cheated people on their taxes, I will give them back four times as much!" (Luke 19:8). This is what prompts Jesus's declaration of salvation. Salvation involves restorative justice. Confession precedes it, but action follows.

Dr. Sandra Glahn further emphasizes action by constructing an interesting story. What if Zacchaeus's exploitation had caused someone to lose their home? After this declaration, the homeless person would be elated! His home, plus further economic remuneration, would follow! In this story, Dr. Glahn calls him Zach. She writes:

> You could not be more thrilled that Zach has new life. And you tell him you cannot wait to get back your old house—the house of your ancestors—not to mention the quadrupled size of the real estate!
>
> And Zach looks stunned. "You actually expect me to give up my house?"
>
> Now it's your turn to be stunned. "But you took possession of it twenty years ago…"
>
> Zach scoffs. "Twenty years! Buddy, you need to lose that 'victim identity' you have going. If that even happened, it was

a *long* time ago. I'm a different person now. Besides, if I had really taken your house and land, why would you wait this long to bring it up? Why would you want to *ruin my life?*"

His callousness only adds to your pain. And you wonder if his God is real. His friends who claim to know God say you must be lying or at fault if you waited this long to say anything. And you wonder if their God is real, too. Their religious friends say anyone who waits a long time to reveal an injustice must be lying or have ulterior motives. And you promise yourself never to go to their house of worship because theirs is not the kind of God who is worthy of your worship.[2]

WOLVES AND JESUS

We forget that Jesus, the one who loved the broken, also had harsh words for those who continued to break others. He called those to account who put heavy burdens on followers. He warned about supposed believers who said one thing and acted predatorily instead. In the same Sermon on the Mount, he warned, "Beware of false prophets who come disguised as harmless sheep but are really vicious wolves" (Matthew 7:15). Wolves, by nature, are animals of prey. But they become even more heinous in the church when wolflike predators don a sheep's pelt. This is why we see an unprecedented number of religious figures harming children and adults within the church. Why? Because the church is a perfect place to hide. It's an institution that engenders trust, which people convey more easily within its four walls. Predatory people (we'll explore this more in chapter 7) are highly skilled at blending in, saying Christian words, and looking upright. They hide their predation with a smile and good community standing. We see this when a known and confessed sexual abuser (pastor) receives a standing ovation for his "confession" of exploiting a minor in his care.

OVATION

The world watches the church and is not likely appreciating what it sees. From the outside it observes a congregation preferring grace over justice, one powerful man's word over the cries of a survivor. I cannot help but wonder what Jesus would do in this situation. Would he stand to his nail-scarred feet, give a pass to the poor pastor who crossed a criminal line, and heartily applaud? Or would he walk out of that church, turning over tables as he left? We have forgotten Jesus's bent toward justice. We prefer cheap grace to the hard-won grace of the cross—itself a symbol of the consequences of sin. Justice matters to the heart of God, and it should matter deeply to the church. Cheap grace nullifies the effects of sin, while genuine grace watches out for the broken cries of the survivor, while bringing to light the sin (and crime) of the one perpetrating.

Jesus's grace is sufficient for all—even perpetrators of sexual abuse. But in matters of justice and oppression and crime? He reminds us to obey our governing authorities (who are best at handling criminal issues), encourages payment of taxes (to fund law enforcement), and jumps out of line in order to pursue the outcasts and unnoticed ones left in the wake of abuse and crimes. I cannot help but imagine Jesus leaving the applause-filled room, finding a sexual abuse survivor, and listening to her story with empathy.

I fear the church has lost the justice side of Jesus. We embrace the image of a Jesus who glosses over perpetration with a grace Band-Aid, and we shy away from the Jesus who asks for radical repentance and restoration (submitting to governing authorities, making amends, participating in restorative justice, not caring about reputation anymore). I'm reminded of the rich young ruler who appeared to do everything right. He said all the right religious words—and quite persuasively— but he lacked one thing. Repentance for him meant forsaking position, power, and wealth in order to radically follow Jesus and give to those in need. Instead, he chose to walk away.

Who suffers when we applaud perpetrators? We all do. Our children do. The vulnerable do. While we can absolutely extend forgiveness and grace to all who repent, this extension does not magically remove the penalty for an offense or erase its effects on the survivor. Nor does it allow perpetrators who are caught to continue on in positions of authority over others, when that very position of authority empowered them to prey on others. Glossing over victimization and using language that minimizes its devastating effect hurts us all.

Remember this: A perpetrator may have hurt someone for a few minutes of his/her life and may even regret it, but a survivor lives with the pain, triggers, shame, and fear for a lifetime. For the perpetrator, it's a passing incident. But for the survivor, it's a life-long battle. It is time we look at the reality of our world and even our church world, where abuse is, sadly, all too common. The church that represents Jesus Christ should be the safest and most restorative place on earth for those who have suffered any kind of abuse. But often, it is not. It is time for this to change—for all our sakes.

GRACE AND TRUTH

A robust theology of grace and truth is needed. We see the marriage of these two concepts in John 1:14: "And the Word became flesh and dwelt among us, and we have seen his glory, glory as of the only Son from the Father, full of grace and truth" (ESV). Both are aspects of Jesus's character, and both are equally important. Emphasize grace without truth, and we see a congregation standing to its feet for a predator. Emphasize truth without grace, and there is no pathway for restoration—for the survivor or the predatory one. Grace plus truth means we call out sin, but we point to the One who bore all sins. Grace plus truth allows for a broken humanity, but it doesn't leave us bleeding on the side of the road. Grace plus truth equals the kingdom of God that Jesus so powerfully and meekly ushered in.

Jesus is the abuse survivor's greatest advocate, most effective healer, and the inaugurator of inevitable justice. He grieves alongside those who grieve, bears the weight of egregious sin perpetrated against the innocent, and has provided a redemptive roadway for us all to travel. At the end of the age, when the new heavens and the new earth dawn, Jesus will be their sole source of light. This is the power of eschatological living: living in expectation of final justice. In that place, at last, "He will wipe every tear from their eyes, and there will be no more death or sorrow or crying or pain. All these things are gone forever"

(Revelation 21:4). Our task until that glorious day is to be the church, the hands and feet and heart and empathy of Jesus to a world in desperate need of healing and light. We are to be agents of his great upside-down kingdom, where outcasts are listened to, the broken are given dignity, and those suffering under the weight of sexual exploitation are rescued and healed.

CHAPTER THREE

ABUSE AND THE CHURCH

*My conclusion from a lifetime of psychohistorical
study of childhood and society is that the history of
humanity is founded upon the abuse of children.*

LLOYD DEMAUSE[1]

S exual abuse runs rampant throughout history simply because sin still holds humankind in its grip. As long as sin flourishes, the exploitation of others will thrive and continue. There is nothing new under the sun, the author of Ecclesiastes tells us, and in the case of assault, deviance has always been with us. We like to think of ourselves as above history or beyond it, but the rampant news cycle reminds us that, yes, even today sexual abuse happens—even in the church (particularly in the church).

But why does sexual abuse happen within our ecclesiastical walls? Shouldn't the church that represents Jesus Christ—the One who loved children and cursed those who harmed them—do the very best job at protecting others from harm? Shouldn't the church be the place a survivor could run in order to be protected, heard, and given restorative justice? Sadly, no. Because so often the church has jumped into bed with power and politics and has given preferential treatment to its reputation instead of the broken cries of survivors.

Steven Mintz recognizes the problem of this marriage of power:

"The problem with the 'psychologizing' of the sexual abuse of minors was the failure to understand the cultures of sexual abuse—including the clerical culture of the Church—which allow abuse to take place. Sexual abuse flourishes in environments with unequal power relationships, particularly when a church's standing in the community is at stake."[2] Sexual abuse always involves the abuse of power and control, and when you have church leaders needing a good communal and national reputation, survivors ultimately take the backseat. Mintz aptly continues:

> Factors that allow sexual abuse to flourish include isolation and social disconnection, both of the abused and the abuser; emotionally needy and disempowered young people; a self-validating ideology that rationalizes abuse; institutional settings that shield individuals from public scrutiny; and institutions intent on protecting their reputation and safeguarding themselves from liability—and that do so in part by decentralizing decision-making about crucial issues.[3]

You'll see this pattern repeated throughout history—a protection-bent clergy or church hierarchy, voiceless victims who don't have collective power to push against the mighty church, and nonexistent pathways of justice. While it would take books upon books to chronicle a wide swath of abuse over the centuries, the following are case studies of how the church has experienced, reacted to, and dealt with abuse in its midst.

SAINT BASIL: A HEART OF JUSTICE

In AD 330, Saint Basil the Great laid out how the church should respond to clerical sexual abuse, demonstrating a heart of justice toward those who harmed the vulnerable and mercy for those harmed. He wrote:

> Any cleric or monk who seduces young men or boys, or who is apprehended in kissing or in any shameful situation,

shall be publicly flogged and shall lose his clerical tonsure. Thus shorn, he shall be disgraced by spitting in his face, bound in iron chains, wasted by six months of close confinement, and for three days each week put on barley bread given him toward evening. Following this period, he shall spend a further six months living in a small segregated courtyard in custody of a spiritual elder, kept busy with manual labor and prayer, subjected to vigils and prayers, forced to walk at all times in the company of two spiritual brothers, never again allowed to associate with young men.[4]

While flogging, spitting, and chains seem to be surprising punishments (though I'm sure some thought it insufficient), removing the clerical tonsure was a correct response—one that Rome has had tremendous difficulty enacting even today. Priests who abused children in their care have been shuffled, not flogged; coddled, not spat upon; empowered, not chained. If the Roman Catholic Church simply revisited the spirit of Saint Basil's words (sans the shaving and starvation for perpetrators), responded to the cries of the broken over the "rights" of the abuser, I doubt we would see the scandal of abuse we're experiencing today.

SAINT PETER DAMIAN ADDRESSES ABUSE

Twelve hundred years later Saint Peter Damian also addressed the issue of priests abusing those in their care. In a letter to Pope Leo IX, he took to task the hierarchical structures that enabled such treachery:

> Listen, you do-nothing superiors of clerics and priests. Listen, and even though you feel sure of yourselves, tremble at the thought that you are partners in the guilt of others; those, I mean, who wink at the sins of their subjects that need correction and who by ill-considered silence allow them license to sin. Listen, I say, and be shrewd enough to understand that all of you alike are deserving of death, that is, not only those who do such things, but also they who approve those who practice them.[5]

Here, Damian not only recognized the clerical depravity, but he also indicated how wrong it was to be a lackadaisical bystander—one who knows about clerical rape and blandly looks the other way. This is in direct violation of Jesus's Good Samaritan story, but the command to actively involve ourselves in matters of injustice extends back to the Old Testament. Rightly, Moses reserves strong language for those who sacrifice their children to the pagan god Molech. But look what he adds: "If the members of the community close their eyes when that man sacrifices one of his children to Molech and if they fail to put him to death, I myself will set my face against him and his family and will cut them off from their people together with all who follow him in prostituting themselves to Molech" (Leviticus 20:3-5 NIV). *If the members of the community close their eyes...*Those who stood by and did nothing? They're equated with those who willingly handed their children over to death. This age-old problem of closing our eyes to abuse has ushered in secondary trauma for many survivors. Sadly, this closing of the eyes continues to be an accepted practice of the church. The first trauma is the sexual assault itself, while the secondary violation is the church's anemic (or absent) response to the allegation. Those who protect perpetrators, knowingly allowing them to repeat their offenses, should be held to high account.

THE REFORMATION'S EFFECTS ON SURVIVORS AND ABUSERS

The cataclysmic effects of the Reformation cannot be underestimated. Besides allowing for clergy marriage, the Protestant Reformation caused the Roman Catholic Church to retreat and reevaluate its power like a lioness licking her wounds. Whereas in previous generations the church tended to move toward protecting survivors and exposing abusers, this openness shifted from transparency to secrecy. Patrick J. Wall writes:

> After the Reformation period, when the Catholic Church effectively lost its monopoly on Christianity, it became more defensive and secretive in order to preserve its power and status. At this time the overall policy towards clergy

sexual abuse returned to the shadows of ecclesiastical clandestiny.[6]

Clearly, the Roman Catholic Church did not want its laity to know of the sexual abuse scandals festering within, more enmeshed with cover-up than investigating the claims of survivors.

POPE BENEDICT XIV PROTECTS PENITENTS

Recently, Father Thomas P. Doyle, along with former monks Richard Sipe and Patrick Wall, wrote a 375-page report entitled "Canonical History of Clerical Sexual Abuse." There they uncovered a startling fact. In 1741, Pope Benedict XIV crafted an important document that

> made it easier to punish priests who solicited sex during confession in exchange for absolution. The tone of the document showed "significant sensitivity to the spiritual damage done to solicited penitents," the authors [Doyle, Sipe, and Wall] wrote. And to ensure the latest church legislation was widely read, the pope ordered it posted on the doors of churches in Rome, including St. Peter's, and at the city's largest market. Those rules became part of the canon law studied by 20th century priests and stayed in force until 1962, when Vatican officials opted for a more secretive process.[7]

SOUTHERN BAPTIST HISTORY OF SLAVERY AND RACISM

Lest we heap all blame at the feet of our Catholic brothers and sisters, it's important to look at the United States' largest Protestant denomination and its slavery-laced history. In the American South, rape was a common occurrence between slave master and slave, though the pervasive fear among Southerners was that black men would rape white women. Because of the power differential between owner and slave, consent could never be reached, and rape became a way of life. Curtis Harris writes,

Much like believing an underage person could consent to sexual relations with an adult, the notion that an enslaved person could consent to any sexual relation with a master is perilously fraught. The plantation system dismantled any notion of consent by the enslaved. Indeed, if there is a central tenet of slavery it is depriving agency from one human and placing it in the craven hands of another. The enslaved who resisted that central tenet risked harsh punishment.[8]

The Southern Baptist denomination roots sink into the issue of slavery. Then, many held the belief that slaveholders were, in fact, missionaries to their slaves and that slavery was a biblical mandate, a necessary institution. One leader, Dr. Richard Furman, wrote this to the governor of South Carolina: "The right of holding slaves is clearly established in the Holy Scriptures, both by precept and example."[9] Some pastors and church leaders participated in the Ku Klux Klan. Much later, in 1956, a South Carolina minister in one of the state's largest Southern Baptist churches spoke before the legislature as a proponent of segregation. It was only in 1995 that Southern Baptist leadership issued a formal apology regarding their support of slavery and inequality for African Americans.[10]

What does this have to do with sexual abuse? Racism and rape deeply scar our history. One particularly shocking case involved 24-year-old Recy Taylor. Six men kidnapped her as she walked home from her Abbeville, Alabama, church and gang raped her. Though one of the rapists confessed to the crime, two white juries refused to convict the accused. This particular case highlighted the seeming lawless nature of the Jim Crow South, but it also fueled an important church-backed movement. Rosa Parks investigated the case, then established the Committee for Equal Justice for Mrs. Recy Taylor. This committee would continue their justice-laden work by organizing the Montgomery Bus Boycotts.

This incident highlights the difficulty of prosecuting rape cases—not only because of jury bias (which is surely deplorable), but also from an evidentiary perspective, as well as anemic statute of limitations laws.

Before the introduction of DNA evidence, rape cases often relied on he said/she said dichotomies. This is certainly the case in date rape, a collegiate epidemic highlighted hauntingly in Jon Krakauer's book *Missoula: Rape and the Justice System in a College Town.* This issue persists—particularly because of the incidence of secondary trauma, where survivors have to publicly retell their stories, and prosecuting a rapist, particularly if he or she is popular, is difficult.

WORLDWIDE SEXUAL ABUSE TODAY

The world continues to see sexual abuse flourish.

- Sex trafficking proliferates at alarming rates. (It's to be noted that the church has led the way in confronting this issue with ministries like the A 21 Campaign, First Aid Arts, and the International Justice Mission leading the way.)

- Pornography, because of the Internet and entropy-like depravity, is constantly available 24/7 in our pockets. Instead of slinking into a creepy building, we can peruse dehumanizing images in the comfort of our own homes.

- Wartime rape accompanies genocide. ISIS kidnaps young girls for the sole purpose of raping virgins.

- Child marriage is common in many countries (and still occurs in the United States).

Add to this the unprecedented rise of sexual abuse allegations in the church, and you have a perfect storm of grief and trauma. In the Catholic Church, priests have been accused of raping young boys and girls for decades—and the only negative consequences pedophile priests experienced was the slight inconvenience of moving, attending redemptive retreats, or being shuffled from diocese to diocese—all secretly. The scandal, still not adequately addressed by the current pope, is widespread—spanning Australia, Germany, France, the Netherlands, Brazil, the United States, Canada, the Dominican Republic, Switzerland, Austria, and Ireland among many other countries.[11]

THE PROTESTANT CHURCH AND SEXUAL ABUSE

Lest we think the Protestant church is immune, recent sexual harassment scandals, including one of the largest and most influential churches in the nation, highlight that the abuse of power is no respecter of persons. Boz Tchividjian, founder of Godly Response to Abuse in Christian Environments (GRACE), had this to say about the Protestant church and the scope of the sexual abuse problem:

> A few years ago, data was gathered from some of the top insurance providers for Protestant churches. It was found that they received 260 reports a year of minors being sexually abused by church leaders or church members...It's important to share that statistic when speaking with Protestant audiences so that they stop pointing their fingers at the Catholic Church and engage more with their own church.[12]

Couple that with the independent nature of Protestant churches, and you find it almost impossible to warn other churches of predatory pastors. There is no nationwide database to consult. Predators have the ability to reinvent themselves, spin a good redemption story, and set up shop in a new locale—with little or no paper trail. In addition, we've exported abuse overseas. Missions organizations, particularly missionary kid schools, have been called out in recent years for deplorable and ongoing sexual abuse.[13] Christian schools have been havens for abusers, as have youth groups. Oversight is often sketchy at best, and many congregations don't have policies and procedures in place to deal with allegations. And so many times, when abuse is exposed, churches retreat to handling the "sin issue" internally rather than obeying the laws of the land and mandatorily reporting it to the proper authorities.

Some theological systems empower abuse. When women are deemed less than, and children have zero rights, and men are seen as the only purveyors of power, there is little space to confront and flee abuse. Those power structures continue to keep the weak subservient to the strong.

THE #METOO MOVEMENT

The #MeToo movement, inaugurated by the tweets of Tarana Burke (who originated the hashtag) and reintroduced by Alyssa Milano in 2017 in the wake of the Harvey Weinstein scandal, introduced a flurry of survivor stories and the downfall of those in power who had preyed on others for years. We're currently seeing an unprecedented shift both in the way we view sexual assault and in how we approach justice in this new age of transparency. The church stands at this intersection, sometimes being a clarion voice for needed change, at other times receding into the background, caring for reputation more than protection of the survivor.

This is where we find ourselves today. Light is breaking through, but the darkness pushes back relentlessly. We have to remember that the battle we face is not against people per se, but against the evil forces behind their heinous actions. This does not mean we avoid prosecuting perpetrators and seeking justice, but it does mean we recall the very real nature of evil in our world. To trace the history of the church's response to sexual abuse through the centuries is to trace the handiwork of Satan, who is alive and well and wants nothing more than to destroy us all. This is a battle that we must fight in the podium and the civil arena, but we also must fight it on our knees. The apostle Paul reminds us as "a final word" in his letter to the Ephesians:

> Be strong in the Lord and in his mighty power. Put on all of God's armor so that you will be able to stand firm against all strategies of the devil. For we are not fighting against flesh-and-blood enemies, but against evil rulers and authorities of the unseen world, against mighty powers in this dark world, and against evil spirits in the heavenly places (Ephesians 6:10-12)

Uncovering sexual abuse is war. Bringing healing is reparative. And being the true body of Christ, including hands, feet, arms, intellect, action, and passion, means both: exposure and healing.

PART TWO

INTERPRETING THE PRESENT

CHAPTER FOUR

THE POWER OF SECRETS

As far back as I can remember, I was sexually abused by my father. I figure I was around 3 years old in some of the earliest memories. Initially, I had no way to know that anything was wrong. When I did eventually come to realize the fact, I had no way to accurately express what was happening to me. There [sic] followed immense shame, distrust and hurt throughout my childhood—even in the happy times. Thus ran the two parallel storylines that became my life.

JESSICA WILLIS FISHER,
former member of the Christian
singing group, *The Willis Clan*[1]

W hen I experienced traumatic and ongoing sexual assault at age five by teenage bullies, I initially kept the secret. Why? Because I experienced what many survivors walk through: fear, terror, and threats. "If you tell anyone," one of the boys told me, "we'll kill your parents." Sean Fallon of the UK, who was abused as a boy by his priest, related a similar phenomenon: "I was too frightened to not do as I was told."[2] So often, sexual assault happens in a context in which the perpetrator is stronger or has more power in the relationship. Fear of what others will think, particularly when the abuse happens within the family structure, in the case for Jessica Willis Fisher above, also keeps survivors silent. No one wants to be the reason for a family's downfall. No one wants to be the linchpin that, when pulled out, unhinges a religious system that is otherwise intact. No one wants to get people in trouble, even if it is necessary to protect yourself.

Even so, sometimes survivors do tell their awful secrets, only to be dismissed, shamed into silence, or flat out ignored. For me? It was the latter. After the boys began inviting their friends to rape me, I knew I had to take charge. Oddly, I didn't feel like my parents would take any protective measures, so I told my babysitter first—a heavyset, chain-smoking woman whose babysitting credentials included a tangible hatred of children. When she said the magic five words, "I will tell your mother," I felt a modicum of relief. Surely the months-long ordeal was completed. My secret now lived in reality, and the perpetrators would no longer attack me, or that's what I naively believed. Five-year-old me had no inclination of justice or that the boys would be taken away by police. I simply envisioned them stopping, where the adults in my life served as a protective barrier to their abuse.

Not so.

The next day after my secret revelation, the boys knocked on the babysitter's door, asked for me, and she pushed me out into the ever-green air to be raped once again under a canopy of Douglas firs. The shock of her push shuddered me. Something inside me died in that moment. Though I could not articulate those thoughts with my trau-matized kindergarten mind, the pernicious belief shot through me: *I am unworthy of protection.* It seemed that not one human being—not a babysitter, not a parent, not even my teacher who must have seen signs of my abuse—could be inconvenienced to take notice of my awful predicament. I was a clever girl, thankfully, and devised a plan on my own—sans adults. I would sleep, feigning the longest marathon naps the world had known because I knew one small fact about my babysit-ter that trumped her awful indifference: She was lazy. And to rouse me on the other side of her house would have been far too much trouble. So as long as I slept through entire afternoons until my mom picked me up around 6:00 p.m., I was safe. I had saved myself.

When, blessedly, we moved at year's end, I felt tremendous relief. I would be safe from those awful boys. But as I've written in other nar-ratives, I felt like I had a "Come molest me" neon sign flashing on my forehead. I spent much of my childhood running from predators. While it would have been better for me to retell my secret and let my mom and stepfather know of my constant, deeply held fears, I kept silent about it. I believed telling someone would have no effect, or that I would be dismissed. To tell my father made little sense either. Though he died when I was ten, for years he had engaged in predatory, grooming behavior toward me and others. Deep down, I must have felt he would have looked at my rape story with ho-hum nonchalance. After all, he continued to take nude pictures of women in compromising poses, hosted naked people at gatherings in his home, and sometimes took pictures of me without clothes. He made me bathe him and told me about sex when I was far too young to be told. It took me ten additional years post-rape to finally tell my story, and then only after I'd met Jesus. Even so, I had to retell the story many times in order to convince folks that it all actually happened.

My story is unusual. Many people take several more decades to share; some never do. This, incidentally, is why the statute of limitations laws must be revamped in our country.

Secrets fester and ruin the lives of the silent. Secrets are powerful and pervasive. They thrive in shame-based systems where perfection is heralded and sin and weakness are covered up. Secrets don't last long in authentic, safe communities, but they multiply in systems—churches, families, sports teams, schools—where reputation matters more than safety.

Consider what happened to Barbara Maasch, which she told 50 years after her abuse. She remembers the pattern of the linoleum floor, the color of the blankets. She was ten years old when she says she was sexually abused by Jamsa, her brother-in-law—who is nearly 20 years older than she is—in his Duluth apartment. She was afraid to speak out at the time, and said she was dismissed when she later found the courage to tell some family members. Maasch was haunted for years by depression and feelings of fear and worthlessness. She twice attempted suicide. "I never felt there was anyone I could go to for protection or help," said Maasch, now 62. "It was just an awful secret...I was too ashamed. I didn't want anyone to have that picture of me, that mental image."[3]

I wonder what would have happened if Barbara felt the freedom to share earlier, or that when she did, the one listening believed her and took redemptive action. How many years of depression and suicidal thoughts could have been alleviated by someone simply listening, caring more for Barbara's soul than the status quo.

Women in war-ravaged countries experience this secrecy on a global scale. One story out of the UK feels particularly heartbreaking, where a girl called Grace (not her real name) had been given in marriage as a child to a powerful man in an African country. She and her sister were systematically raped and forced to participate in creepy rituals to supposedly increase their husband's status. An uncle arranged for them to flee to the UK, where Grace continued to be raped by the men in church families that took her in.

> At the age of 37, Grace has never had consensual sex. "I am not the only one. There are many more women like me," she says, hunched over and looking down at the table. She indicates to the wall that separates the small meeting room from her friends in the adjacent room. "We are the most destitute and vulnerable women in the UK."[4]

Some keep secrets because they have to in order to survive.

Some 35 percent of women globally have experienced some form of sexual violence, though because of the nature of secrets, this number is most likely underreported. For some countries, the statistics are even more shocking: 57 percent of Bangladeshi women, 77 percent of Cambodian women, 79 percent of Indian women, 87 percent of Vietnamese women, and 99 percent of Egyptian women have experienced some form of sexual harassment—which involves innuendo, inappropriate comments, and unwanted sexual solicitation. One hundred twenty million girls globally have experienced forced sex. Seven hundred fifty million girls will be married before their eighteenth birthday.[5] The most commonly cited US statistic for women is that one in four women have been assaulted, with 65 percent reporting incidents of sexual harassment.[6] Because of secrecy and the stigma attached to male exploitation, the statistics for male survivors is underrepresented.

The commonly held statistic in the US is one in six men have experienced sexual abuse or rape. A 1998 report showed male sexual abuse is "common, under-reported, under-recognized, and under-treated."[7] Why all the silence? Why keep these awful secrets? An untold story never heals. Letting our stories out into the light of day with a safe person is the first step toward wholeness. It certainly was for me, even though it took me several attempts to convince the adults in my life that it did, in fact, happen. In sharing about the abuse, I was able to see that I was not at fault for the abuse. I began to understand how the rapes had affected me, and I experienced the power of someone else shouldering my narrative—a story that had weighed my soul down with depression and constant suicidal thoughts. I would not be alive, I'm convinced, had I not let out my story. Eventually, it would have destroyed me.

Knowing the benefits of releasing their secrets, why do people keep stories to themselves? Seven reasons:

THE SYSTEM PREVENTS IT

In highly patriarchal church, ministry, and family systems, what matters most is the social standing of the institution in the midst of culture. These systems are to be a beacon, a ray of hope, untainted by sin or nefarious practices. To expose the flaws in the system is to invite the wrath of that system upon oneself. The stakes are particularly high: If you talk, you'll lose every important relationship you have. If you disclose, you'll ruin the reputation of the system, and any sort of fallout will not be the perpetrator's fault, but yours. All that blame will be heaped upon you. That fear drives many to silence, though the abuse (even after it's over) has a way of eating up the silent one cancerously.

SHAME

Shame is a powerful force that causes abuse survivors to heap blame upon themselves for someone else's predation. More often than not, the shame that should be reserved for the one violating another is internalized, instead, by the survivor. Second-guessing is common. *Maybe*

I wanted it? Maybe I gave off some sort of vibe to invite those advances? Maybe there's something fundamentally wrong with me to attract such attention? When enslaved to shame, survivors begin to believe the horrific voices in their heads shouting their worthlessness. So, if a survivor finally tells the world (or even a close friend) what happened, he/she will simply be proving what society must have thought all along: Survivors are dirty, broken, unworthy. To have been abused proves our powerlessness; it proves that we didn't prevail in protecting ourselves.

A HAPPY WORLD

Living in denial, though seemingly inactive, is an explosive action. By it, we misrepresent the past in order to create a better world for ourselves. To admit we were harmed is to admit our failure to protect ourselves. So we minimize and rationalize someone else's bad behavior as "no big deal" so we can go back to living in a happy world where nothing bad happens to anyone. When we say, "What I experienced was no big deal," we are actively trying to convince ourselves that we should be fine, we *are* fine, while downplaying the very real specter of trauma that haunts us when we're lying in bed awake at night. We can even rationalize on behalf of our abuser, giving excuses that he or she has had a hard life, and perhaps we were simply overreacting. This keeps the happy world in place, where predatory behavior is relegated to a mild misdemeanor; our reactions must accordingly be stuffed and wrangled, and everyone can carry on with their normal life.

REPERCUSSIONS

Many people keep secrets to keep the status quo. If they speak, they will suffer the consequences. We've certainly seen that in the #MeToo stories, where women and men lost their jobs or advancement opportunities for standing up for themselves or leaking their stories. Those who would face economic crisis as a result of speaking out usually have little or no appetite for reporting abuse because it would mean a loss of livelihood for their families. For many in service industries, the choice is between silence and abject poverty. But not only that, people who are lacking in power also fear that the powerful person who abuses will continue to abuse them in different ways—by filing lawsuits, verbal harassment, or even stalking their prey.

LEARNED HELPLESSNESS

Dr. Martin Seligman coined the term "learned helplessness" to describe what happens to many trauma survivors. The phenomenon occurs when we begin to believe that our actions and reactions have no impact on our future. If we've continually tried to remedy a situation, only to fail and fail again, we'll internalize this helplessness. Trying to grab at control only ends in nothing, so why try? I certainly experienced this when I was repeatedly raped at five. I began to believe no one would help me, and though I learned the art of napping, internally I continued to believe that nothing would ever change, and that terrible things were always about to happen to me. When abuse survivors are entrenched in learned helplessness, they begin to argue with themselves, *Why even tell? Nothing will happen. No one will believe me. It's too late anyway. And if I tell, something even worse is bound to happen.*

THE NATURE OF TRAUMA

Many don't tell their secrets because of the nature of trauma. There are many in-the-moment responses to trauma. Survivors may fight, fly, fawn, or freeze. The latter two are reasons a survivor may keep their secret—because they feel they responded inappropriately to unwanted sexual advances. They may shame themselves for not fighting back, not realizing that the typical response is actually to fawn (feign acceptance until it's over, hopefully quickly) or freeze. Survivors play their abuse scenario over and over in their minds, reminding themselves of the times they could have fled but did not. They worry that if they tell someone what happened, the first question they'll receive in retort is, "Well, why didn't you just fight back or run away?" And, sadly, many survivors have heard this response, or even more insufferable: "If that were me, I would have kicked him where it counts."

We are so desperately unschooled when it comes to complex trauma—survivors keep secrets for so long because often responses of those they tell are both ignorant of how trauma works and self-righteously judgmental.

THREATS

At times, survivors of sexual abuse do not tell their stories because the victimizer, those protecting the perpetrator, or the system to which the perpetrator belongs have threatened violence, public humiliation, lawsuits, or some sort of veiled threat. I truly believed that the teenage rapists meant what they said, that they would murder my parents if I let the secret slip (and I am still surprised I told my babysitter, knowing my fear). Some survivors keep secrets for decades because the threat looms large—even after a perpetrator has died. Underneath all this lies shame. Some survivors of sexual abuse tell themselves that if they tell anyone, they will be knowingly inviting more violence or verbal harm against themselves. Their threats became a warning that puts the survivor in charge of the consequences. If survivors keep silent, threats won't materialize. If survivors talk, threats ensue.

We see the raw power and pervasiveness of secrets when we look at the Catholic clergy sex abuse scandal, where thousands of survivors kept silent for decades. Some bravely tried to tell. Some parents raised a ruckus. Some people tried to do the right thing, but by and large, the secrets stayed secret, while pedophile priests were shuffled from one preying ground to another, preserving the institution while marginalizing the laity. The effects on countless devastated lives are just beginning to emerge. Secrets have a way of worming their way from darkness to light. As Jesus reminded us:

> Don't be afraid of those who threaten you. For the time is coming when everything that is covered will be revealed, and all that is secret will be made known to all. What I

tell you now in the darkness, shout abroad when daybreak comes. What I whisper in your ear, shout from the house-tops for all to hear! Don't be afraid of those who want to kill your body; they cannot touch your soul. Fear only God, who can destroy both soul and body in hell (Matthew 10:26-28).

God does see. He knows. And while it may be cold comfort today, in the muck of pain, to know that *someday* all wrongs will be dealt with justly, it is a solid truth we can rest in when lies and cover-ups prevail.

As faith communities, it is imperative that we reflect on these seven reasons why people keep sexual abuse secrets, and then take active measures to remedy them. We can become open systems with nothing to hide. We can choose to believe the cry of the survivor over the protestations of abusers. We can provide safe places for abuse survivors to share their stories, through tears and shaking. We can offer counseling services, recovery programs, walk-alongside ministries, small group care, and genuine empathy. We can educate ourselves about trauma and the awful aftereffects of rape, abuse, violence, and harassment. We can become openhearted havens that represent the best of Jesus, welcoming secrets while offering solace.

CHAPTER FIVE

THE PERSUASIVENESS OF BAD THEOLOGY

The cross is the ultimate repudiation of the idea that power is to be wielded for the benefit and pleasure of those who possess it.

RACHAEL DENHOLLANDER[1]

Theology has to grapple with the reality of our sin-soiled world and the nature of our triune God. When either is misrepresented, we tread dangerous waters. What we think about humanity matters. What we think about God matters. And what we think as a church naturally fuels our actions. If we believe God has biblically mandated humankind to own slaves, we will either own slaves or not intervene when our ostensibly God-fearing neighbor does. If we believe some lives are more important than others, we will callously look the other way when those who are considered less-than are marginalized. The sexual abuse crisis in the church has its roots in incomplete theology, sinful practices, and a misunderstanding of the nature of evil and God's justice.

INCOMPLETE THEOLOGY

Rachael Denhollander, the first gymnast to publicly tell her story of abuse by Larry Nassar, agrees that incomplete theologies allow for the current crisis:

> You have that dynamic with evangelical churches where you have the reputation on the line and the perceived

reputation of the gospel of Christ. But often, if not always, people are motivated by poor theology and a poor understanding of grace and repentance and that causes them to handle sexual assault in a way that a lot of predators go unchecked, often for decades. When you see a theological commitment to handling sexual assault inappropriately, you have the least hope of ever changing it.[2]

Any theology that subverts the idea of *imago dei,* that we all bear the image of God as his created children, allows for the mistreatment of others as justifiable or tolerable. Genesis 1:27 reminds us of this central truth: "So God created human beings in his own image. In the image of God he created them; male and female he created them." Both men and women are image bearers, and we carry the weight of God around in our mortal bodies, the immortal shining through human skin. We are the result of a triune God's self-emptying love. Before our world took on soil, sky, oceans, and wildlife, our relational God existed in threefold mysterious relationship, hovering over the darkness, sufficient in himself. He is love codified, a beautiful internal relationship that endeavored to create mankind from that harmony of fellowship. We are his children, and he is our divine parent. This thought is continued in the New Testament: "In him we live and move and exist. As some of your own poets have said, 'We are his offspring'" (Acts 17:28).

Just as parents grieve when their children hurt each other, God must grieve when his children exploit one another, sexually assault the helpless, and traffic children for prostitution. Have you considered the grief of God as he looks upon this earth? How his heart must ache from our choices! We see the grief of God prior to Noah's ark-making, when the earth was filled with unrelenting violence. God's heart throughout the history of the nation of Israel was to woo humanity back to himself—a relationship that was forever altered in the garden when the first human beings chose the lure of knowing good and evil over relationship with the only One who was good. Israel was to be a light shining in the darkness, a vehicle for wooing a broken humanity back to the One who created them.

Attention to the imagery of light reveals the story of God throughout the testaments, and this frequent metaphor peppers the pages of Scripture. Prior to the creation of humanity, God said, "'Let there be light,' and there was light" (Genesis 1:3). Post-flood, God inaugurated his first great commission when he called Abraham to leave his home and become a great nation (see Genesis 12). Throughout the Old Testament, we see admonitions that this new nation was to protect the helpless, care for the poor, support the widow, and extend kindness to aliens. This power differential that existed in the world was not intended for exploitation, but service. Those who found themselves in positions of power were to judge fairly, love widely, and create a just society. All this hinted at a future glory, when God himself would send the Son to continue this practice publicly.

In the meantime, God's heart bent toward the broken. His intent was to bring all humankind into relationship with himself, and he often aligned himself with the downtrodden. If Israel harmed those who were deemed "the least," they would rile the heart of God. Consider this warning in Psalm 12:5 (NIV): "'Because the poor are plundered and the needy groan, I will now arise,' says the LORD. 'I will protect them from those who malign them.'" The prophet Zechariah prophesied against those who refused God's command to protect the innocent and downtrodden:

> Then this message came to Zechariah from the LORD: "This is what the LORD of Heaven's Armies says: Judge fairly, and show mercy and kindness to one another. Do not oppress widows, orphans, foreigners, and the poor. And do not scheme against each other. Your ancestors refused to listen to this message. They stubbornly turned away and put their fingers in their ears to keep from hearing. They made their hearts as hard as stone, so they could not hear the instructions or the messages that the LORD of Heaven's Armies had sent them by his Spirit through the earlier prophets. That is why the LORD of Heaven's Armies was so angry with them" (Zechariah 7:8-12).

It's important to note that orphans and the poor were in perilous danger of being exploited in every possible way, even sexually. These outcasts bore the *imago dei*, but so often Israel held on to its peculiar relationship with God as something to lord over others rather than to act justly, love mercy, and walk humbly with their God (see Micah 6:8).

Darkness prevailed for many on the earth, whether in the time of the patriarchs, the cycle of judges, the kingly rule of David (and following), or the era of prophets. Yet light, in its persistent beauty, continued to woo and beckon the nation back to the One who created it. We see this extensively in the book of Isaiah, a beautiful now-and-not-yet book that revealed what happened in the nation at the moment (and God's heartbeat behind it), while coaxing toward what would be—a Messiah who would come to inaugurate a new kingdom. He says, "You will do more than restore the people of Israel to me. I will make you a light to the Gentiles, and you will bring my salvation to the ends of the earth" (Isaiah 49:6). You can almost hear the longing of God in this verse, this great unveiling of the progression of his plan of salvation: "Arise, Jerusalem! Let your light shine for all to see. For the glory of the Lord rises to shine on you. Darkness as black as night covers all the nations of the earth, but the glory of the Lord rises and appears over you. All nations will come to your light; mighty kings will come to see your radiance" (Isaiah 60:1-3). This light-bearing mandate prepared Israel to meet her king, Jesus. Isaiah prophesied, "The people who walk in darkness will see a great light. For those who live in a land of deep darkness, a light will shine" (Isaiah 9:2).

Throughout the New Testament, we see Jesus as the light-carrier, ushering in a new era of love and kindness (and, yes, justice). Matthew quotes the verses from Isaiah when he writes, "The people who sat in darkness have seen a great light. And for those who lived in the land where death casts its shadow, a light has shined" (Matthew 4:16). We see the Trinitarian God break into history in a flash of love-empowered light in John's opening narrative:

> In the beginning the Word already existed. The Word was with God, and the Word was God. He existed in the

beginning with God. God created everything through him, and nothing was created except through him. The Word gave life to everything that was created, and his life brought light to everyone. The light shines in the darkness, and the darkness can never extinguish it (John 1:1-5).

Note the word "everyone." Not some. Not merely those the world favored as important, but all who bear the image of the almighty, all-caring, all-seeing God.

Everyone.

Even the victimized.

To those who felt that God stood far away from their plight, Jesus gave this powerful reminder: "I am the light of the world. If you follow me, you won't have to walk in darkness, because you will have the light that leads to life" (John 8:12). In the following chapter of John, we see a powerful interaction with a man born blind. If I could create a patron saint of the sexually abused, it would be him, as he experienced survivor-blaming by the disciples—sadly, something nearly every sexual abuse survivor has heard. "As Jesus was walking along, he saw a man who had been blind from birth. 'Rabbi,' his disciples asked him, 'why was this man born blind? Was it because of his own sins or his parents' sins?'" (John 9:1-2). Here's a man who did not cause his own blindness, whose station in life was precarious at best because of this condition. He didn't beckon it, want it, or "deserve" it. I feel his predicament in my gut. Surely, if I could have chosen *not* to be sexually assaulted, I would have chosen that. But the fact remains, I have been. And the fact for this man is that he was blind.

Note what Jesus says here, and the way he skillfully weaves in the light metaphor. "'It was not because of his sins or his parents' sins,' Jesus answered. 'This happened so the power of God could be seen in him. We must quickly carry out the tasks assigned us by the one who sent us. The night is coming, and then no one can work. But while I am here in the world, I am the light of the world'" (John 9:3-5). He then heals the man, which causes further discord with the Pharisees. We are tasked with a similar mandate to carry out the tasks Jesus has given us: to love the least, the last, and the lost by not assigning blame, but instead becoming agents of healing and restoration.

Sin, we know, is darkness—a theme we will explore in the next section, but it's interesting to note that when Jesus bore the weight of every sin (including rape, sexual exploitation, harassment, deviance, and trafficking), the day turned to night: "By this time it was about noon, and darkness fell across the whole land until three o'clock. The light from the sun was gone. And suddenly, the curtain in the sanctuary of the Temple was torn down the middle. Then Jesus shouted, 'Father, I entrust my spirit into your hands!' And with those words he breathed his last" (Luke 23:44-46). The light of the world bled, died, and plunged the world into an even greater darkness for three terrible days—days where darkness seemed to prevail, sin appearing to be victorious, while the demonic cackled their win.

But light erupted from the inky darkness! God raised Jesus to life! What a powerful picture to absorb that the first witnesses of the resurrection of Jesus were women—Mary Magdalene, Joanna, Mary the mother of James, and several other women according to the Scriptures. Once again, we see glorious light, while second-class citizens (women) were given the audacious first look at life conquering death once and for all.

> As they stood there puzzled, two men suddenly appeared to them, clothed in dazzling robes. The women were terrified and bowed with their faces to the ground. Then the men asked, "Why are you looking among the dead for someone who is alive? He isn't here! He is risen from the dead! Remember what he told you back in Galilee, that the Son of Man must be betrayed into the hands of sinful men and be crucified, and that he would rise again on the third day" (Luke 24:4-7).

Note the dazzling splendor of the moment. Light. Joy. A risen Savior!

Throughout the New Testament, we continue to see the imagery of light. As children of light, we are to walk in a manner worthy of this light—particularly in the way we treat those who are broken. Ephesians 5 is a careful road map of what living in the light means. We are to love well and turn away from sexual immorality (among other self-aggrandizing sins). Paul warns:

> Don't be fooled by those who try to excuse these sins, for the anger of God will fall on all who disobey him. Don't participate in the things these people do. For once you were full of darkness, but now you have light from the Lord. So live as people of light! For this light within you produces only what is good and right and true. Carefully determine what pleases the Lord. Take no part in the worthless deeds of evil and darkness; instead, expose them. It is shameful even to talk about the things that ungodly people do in secret. But their evil intentions will be exposed when the light shines on them, for the light makes everything visible. This is why it is said, "Awake, O sleeper, rise up from the dead, and Christ will give you light" (Ephesians 5:6-14).

With a robust theology of light, we must not only shun sexual violence, but expose it while ensuring it doesn't propagate. We are to bring justice for both survivors and perpetrators. Any sort of cover-up is partnering with darkness and originates from the father of lies.

Isaiah looks toward Jesus and the revelation of the new heavens and the new earth when he prophesies:

> No longer will you need the sun to shine by day, nor the moon to give its light by night, for the LORD your God will be your everlasting light, and your God will be your glory. Your sun will never set; your moon will not go down. For the LORD will be your everlasting light. Your days of mourning will come to an end. All your people will be righteous. They will possess their land forever, for I will plant them there with my own hands in order to bring myself glory. The smallest family will become a thousand people, and the tiniest group will become a mighty nation. At the right time, I, the LORD, will make it happen (Isaiah 60:19-22).

Living with an eschatological mindset, though difficult, reminds us that, in the end, darkness will be extinguished, and light will prevail. Those who consider themselves "the smallest" will see fruition, and, in the very end, all tears will be dried. This is pure hope for the one who has spent a life being victimized, silenced, and harmed. As the church, we are to represent this very real light to those who are harmed, and the extent to which we don't rise up is the extent to which the broken will be further broken. We are light bearers, but when we overlook the cries of the marginalized, we align ourselves with an agenda of darkness.

God started our world with light. He asked Israel to be a beacon of light to the nations, then fulfilled his promise of light by sending his Son as a sacrifice for our sins. We now bear the heritage of Jesus, continuing the mandate of light-carrying to a sin-blackened world. And someday, on the shores of eternity, we will no longer need the lesser sun to illuminate us. Blessedly, we will be set free from the darkness. As the apostle John put it in his glorious vision of heaven,

> I saw no temple in the city, for the Lord God Almighty and the Lamb are its temple. And the city has no need of sun or moon, for the glory of God illuminates the city, and the Lamb is its light. The nations will walk in its light, and the kings of the world will enter the city in all their glory. Its gates will never be closed at the end of day because there is no night there (Revelation 21:22-25).

As image bearers, we are children of light. Consider Peter's words as our holy mandate: "You are a chosen people. You are royal priests, a holy nation, God's very own possession. As a result, you can show others the goodness of God, for he called you out of the darkness into his wonderful light" (1 Peter 2:9). We've been called from the shadows for such a time as this, carrying the mantle of Queen Esther, who intervened for a nation on the brink of annihilation. There are millions of sexual abuse survivors longing for Esthers (her name means both "compassion" and "star"—an entity that shines in the midnight sky), whose souls are on the brink of annihilation.

SINFUL PRACTICES

It seems obvious to say that sinful practices are party to our current sexual abuse crisis. Of course, we find ourselves in this crisis because there are people who have abused positions of authority and power in order to destroy the vulnerable. But we're also in this crisis because of cover-ups and the silencing of survivors. We do live in a terribly broken world, and sexual sin abounds in every corner of our world. With the proliferation of debauchery in the form of lucrative industries like pornography and sex trafficking, sometimes it feels like we're fighting an unwinnable battle. The church is the hands and feet of Jesus, and it is our duty to continue the mandate to protect the innocent, while turning perpetrators in to the proper authorities. Through the power of the Holy Spirit, we are to shed light on the darkness. But pride and greed keep many silent. Pride over the reputation of the institution or the position of clergy. Greed over the inevitable financial fallout that could occur when people find out and leave the pews. The church's deliberate muteness has allowed for the industry of sexual abuse to flourish unimpeded.

Our world is reminiscent of the one described by Paul in Romans 1, where people have abandoned the God of light and preferred deeds that flourish in the darkness: "So God abandoned them to do whatever shameful things their hearts desired. As a result, they did vile and degrading things with each other's bodies. They traded the truth about God for a lie. So they worshiped and served the things God created instead of the Creator himself, who is worthy of eternal praise! Amen" (Romans 1:24-25). A simple theology of light and darkness helps us understand our current state. John 3:19 reminds us of humankind's bent away from God and toward darkness: "The judgment is based on this fact: God's light came into the world, but people loved the darkness more than the light, for their actions were evil."

Obviously, living in the light means forsaking darkness. And when we choose to live in the light, with the Holy Spirit invigorating our relationships, we will once again exemplify our relational God. We will know and love one another, preferring each other, serving the needy in our midst. Love is the obvious consequence of living in the light.

But sexual abuse thrives in darkness, destroying another image bearer of God through debauchery, sexual license, and unbridled selfishness. John again returns to this metaphor of light:

> This is the message we heard from Jesus and now declare to you: God is light, and there is no darkness in him at all. So we are lying if we say we have fellowship with God but go on living in spiritual darkness; we are not practicing the truth. But if we are living in the light, as God is in the light, then we have fellowship with each other, and the blood of Jesus, his Son, cleanses us from all sin. If we claim we have no sin, we are only fooling ourselves and not living in the truth. But if we confess our sins to him, he is faithful and just to forgive us our sins and to cleanse us from all wickedness (1 John 1:5-9).

There is a communal aspect to these verses. Confession is not done in isolation, but in public with other believers. When fellowship is broken, we are to confess one to another. But so often when it comes to sexual offense, the abuser is protected by the church and shuffled away, while the hard work of forgiving is demanded of the survivor. Seldom do we see a church deal honestly with the crime of sexual abuse from the pulpit. Similarly, we rarely see the church hand over a church-employed perpetrator to the proper authorities. We prefer darkness, reputation, and money to light, God's fame, and trusting him to provide for us when we dare to tell the truth.

We live in a world of entropy, moving from disorder to further disorder, as sexual deviance becomes profoundly mainstream. With this normalization of deviance, perpetrators need more and more prey to whet their abhorrent appetites. The church, if properly aligned with the God of light, should take on the mantle of exposing these deeds of darkness—without hesitation or fear. This is part of our spiritual warfare. It is our duty. Protecting the unprotected, caring for the vulnerable, and becoming part of the solution rather than the problem will be the very thing that helps others take tentative steps back into our churches. To cover up, make excuses, and minimize abuse is to alienate the very people Jesus wants us to reach.

MISUNDERSTANDING OF THE NATURE OF EVIL AND GOD'S JUSTICE

We forget the depth of evil. Evil is pervasive, consuming, and arises as a stench from the pit of hell. Jesus bore it on his perfect shoulders in order to vanquish its proliferation. He conquered death, substituting his life for ours in order to rescue us from iniquity's grip. Sin matters to the Almighty God. Adam and Eve's original sin obliterated humankind's relationship with our holy God, but God's redemptive plan of light played out on the stage of the Bible—for his glory and our saving.

We must not take the cross lightly. We must not cheapen grace by offering it flippantly to those who have plotted to harm the innocence of others. We must not forget the language of Jesus who condemned those who oppressed others. We must face evil as it is, not playing it down or prettying it up. Nor must we forget that sins against humanity (theft, murder, rape), in addition to being sins, are *crimes* too. We are quick to let clichés roll off the tongue, saying things like "all sin is equal." But by equating gossip with rape, we cheapen the very dire consequences to the survivor, and we prevent justice from being served according to Romans 13, where Paul reminds us to submit to the laws of our land. Rape, sexual abuse, and even sexual harassment are crimes, and they are best dealt with by professionals in law enforcement. Does this mean there's no hope for a rapist? No. The gospel always offers hope for the truly repentant, but it is also good news precisely because Jesus took seriously the nature of sin. The gospel doesn't dismiss sin. It pays for it with blood—the most precious commodity a human has.

When we downplay sexual assault, we lessen the torment of evil. When we minimize abuse, we further harm the survivors who have paid for their trauma with flashbacks, triggers, and a host of pain-scarred aftermaths. We do survivors and society a disservice by dismissing a sexual predator's actions as a benign mistake, or what all men fantasize about, or as taking place so long ago that they count simply as a youthful indiscretion. Novelist Ted Dekker wrote something that has stuck with me for many years. He wrote of the importance of characterizing evil for what it was: pure, awful darkness. If we downplay it, redemption cannot shine as brightly. He writes, "I refuse to become complicit with evil by characterizing that nasty, nasty stuff in a way that softens its destructive bite. Doing so would not only be deceptive but it would undermine the great victory won by our hero in his majestic defeat of this terrible villain called evil."[3]

If we minimize sin and crime against others, we minimize the cross. Rachael Denhollander and her husband, Jacob, now advocates, write this: "Christian responses which minimize the evil of abuse have in turn minimized the righteousness and holiness of God."[4] They continue, "At the cross, God acts for others—to overcome evil, uphold justice, free the enslaved, and restore creation. God himself perfectly identifies with the victim because he himself has willingly subjected himself to injustice. The cross is the ultimate repudiation of the idea that power is to be wielded for the benefit and pleasure of those who possess it."[5] Rachael ushered in countless stories of abuse by being the first break in the dam of allegations that continue to pour out against Larry Nassar. As I write this, there are well over 400 known survivors of the pedophile. Cover-up within the USA gymnastics system and the university that employed Nassar are now exposed, but only after years and years of denial, enabling, and empowering a man who will die in prison for his crimes. The Denhollanders write, "To minimize or hide abuse out of concern for reputations, money, influence, or mere apathy and a desire to not get involved is to utterly repudiate the witness of Christ."[6]

We forget that God is a God of justice to our peril. Jesus didn't turn over the tables in the temple as a temper tantrum, but as a demonstration of how much he hated (yes, hated!) injustice, particularly when people profited from the exploitation of the vulnerable. Covering up abuse in the church certainly has an economic element to it, but the sad reality is that, in the long run, the church will suffer far more financially because of all the hiding and the cover-up. People hate hypocrisy, as they should. They don't want to be part of a system that protects perpetrators in order to keep reputations intact falsely and coffers filled deceitfully.

Recently, I had a lively conversation with my friend Charissa, a lawyer who performs investigations for GRACE (Godly Response to Abuse in Christian Environments) on behalf of churches, ministries, missions organizations, and Christian universities. She investigates sexual abuse and how those institutions responded. Sadly, many fail to protect victims, falling into the familiar pattern of institutional protectionism. She reminded me of Psalm 109—a psalm that probably won't make it on a Christian mug or throw blanket. But it's there, stark on the page, written by King David. It's a song of justice, a worship hymn we would most likely not be allowed to sing in the modern church. Let the words shock you back to the issues of justice. Yes, yes, our God is love, but part of that love involves protecting and taking care of everyone who bears his image. Justice and love hold hands.

The psalm begins, "O God, whom I praise, don't stand silent and aloof while the wicked slander me and tell lies about me. They surround me with hateful words and fight against me for no reason. I love them, but they try to destroy me with accusations even as I am praying for them! They repay evil for good, and hatred for my love" (Psalm 109:1-5). In verses 6-19, we see what David's enemies want to do to him, even though he is not to blame. These enemies want accusers to be sent so he'll be pronounced guilty. They ask that his prayers be counted as sins. They advocate for an early death so his children will be fatherless and his wife a widow. They long for a stripping of his position and the repossession of his possessions. No more legacy, they cry! No more reputation! Let him be destroyed. Sadly, this is what happens to many abuse survivors when they dare to come forward. Those being accused do everything they can to destroy them.

David's response reveals the depth of pain caused by the accused hurling accusations:

> May those curses become the LORD's punishment for my accusers who speak evil of me. But deal well with me, O Sovereign LORD, for the sake of your own reputation! Rescue me because you are so faithful and good. For I am poor and needy, and my heart is full of pain. I am fading like a shadow at dusk; I am brushed off like a locust. My knees are weak from fasting, and I am skin and bones. I am a joke to people everywhere; when they see me, they shake their heads in scorn (Psalm 109:20-25).

His words are the cry of so many who have been wounded by others. He ends the psalm with these powerful words, "For he stands beside the needy, ready to save them from those who condemn them" (Psalm 109:31).

David's imprecatory psalm allows full vent to what these mockers say, giving us a revealing picture of those who cover up abuse. They are the ones to whom David assigns disgrace: "May my accusers be clothed with disgrace," he writes (Psalm 109:29). We hear echoes of Tamar in these words, when she rightly asks, "Where could I get rid of my disgrace?" (2 Samuel 13:13 NIV). She who had been violently unclothed by Amnon knows she will carry disgrace for a lifetime; but, in reality, it is those who have perpetrated these foul deeds who walk in disgrace.

Our just and loving God provides the good news of the gospel for all—for both perpetrator and survivor, for those who cover up, and those who are unjustly uncovered. For the victimized, he offers solace and healing. He gives us, the church, the mandate to act on behalf of the broken (oh, that we might fulfill this mandate with relentless verve!), and to the authorities he gives the charge of upholding the law. Our Jesus welcomes predatory people too, his bleeding arms spread wide, just as he welcomed the thieves crucified alongside him. One mocked and missed paradise, while the other admitted his sin and entered into the hereafter justified. But that pathway involved a clear, humble recognition of sin—something that few predators manage. It can happen, but it's not common.

As we will study in the chapter about predators (chapter 7), wolves don't transform into sheep. They seldom turn from their predatory ways; instead, they deceive by donning an innocuously fuzzy pelt, slipping in amidst the flock. It's our job to discern the wolves and separate them from an innocent flock—and continue to do so until the return of Christ. Jesus continually warns his people of this phenomenon—that those who prey are held hostage by evil, yet he is the protector of the vulnerable:

> The thief's purpose is to steal and kill and destroy. My purpose is to give them a rich and satisfying life. I am the

good shepherd. The good shepherd sacrifices his life for the sheep. A hired hand will run when he sees a wolf coming. He will abandon the sheep because they don't belong to him and he isn't their shepherd. And so the wolf attacks them and scatters the flock (John 10:10-12).

A good shepherd doesn't spend his time chasing after wolves and trying to make them into nonpredatory animals. No, he inconveniences himself, sacrificing his own body for the sake of the flock. This is precisely what Jesus did—sacrificing his life for the sake of us all. If we say we love and follow him, we should do the same.

CHAPTER SIX

THE PERVASIVENESS OF PORN

For the world offers only a craving for physical pleasure, a craving for
everything we see, and pride in our achievements and possessions.
These are not from the Father, but are from this world.

1 JOHN 2:16

It's everywhere, this menace. Used to be folks had to sneak a magazine from a relative's stash or go to a creepy place on the other side of town to view it, but now—pornography is in the rectangle in our pockets and purses. Like opiates, porn is addictive, causing those enslaved to need more and more intense forms of deviance to provide the craved dopamine rush. We must understand that this epidemic is ruining lives—certainly the lives of those who view it, but also the lives of those who create it, profit from it, and undoubtedly those enslaved to perform in it. I remember being bothered by the casual references to porn in nearly every episode of the sitcom *Friends*, and a similar laissez-faire attitude continues today. No big deal. Ho hum. A harmless obsession—except that it's not.

THE ROOT

The Greek word *porneia* occurs 26 times in the New Testament, and is the origin of the word we use today. The term is primarily related to fornication—any sexual intercourse outside of marriage—but it also has an interesting connotation. Metaphorically, it can be used to refer to the worship of idols.

As I've written previously, "An idol is something with which you replace God. It can become a foothold Satan uses to climb his way into your affections. It's something you fill yourself up with, revere, pay homage to. Tim Keller wrote, 'Idolatry is always the reason we ever do anything wrong.'"[1,2] Throughout the Old and New Testaments we see the equation of idolatry and the worship of demons. Psalm 106 is a good example:

> They [the Israelites] worshiped their idols, which led to their downfall. They even sacrificed their sons and their daughters to the demons. They shed innocent blood, the blood of their sons and daughters. By sacrificing them to the idols of Canaan, they polluted the land with murder. They defiled themselves by their evil deeds, and their love of idols was adultery in the LORD's sight (verses 36-39).

Take note of how this idolatry harmed children. Paul reminds the Corinthian believers of this same correlation:

> What am I trying to say? Am I saying that food offered to idols has some significance, or that idols are real gods? No, not at all. I am saying that these sacrifices are offered to demons, not to God. And I don't want you to partici-pate with demons. You cannot drink from the cup of the Lord and from the cup of demons, too. You cannot eat at the Lord's Table and at the table of demons, too. What? Do we dare to rouse the Lord's jealousy? Do you think we are stronger than he is? (1 Corinthians 10:19-22).

When we understand the nature of Satan, the one who wants to crush the image bearers of God (all of us), we can see how easily porn fits into his glove of destruction. Why? Because who we are deeply informs our sexuality. Since we are image bearers of our Creator, Satan will do everything to subvert that inheritance, including creating an elaborate, yet destructive counterfeit to our true identity. If he can enslave others to the idolatry of pornography, he not only cuts off our spiritual legs, but, like an idol, he cleverly turns our affections to what is less than—our base desires.

We think happiness and joy come when we indulge our desires, but our eyes deceive us. Our culture promotes this type of "If I want it, then I should have it" mentality, wooing us toward more and more idolatry until we're entangled by secrecy, shame, and powerlessness. The "god" of our appetite lets us down every single time. Paul warns about this slippery slide toward the enemy's plans: "I have told you often before, and I say it again with tears in my eyes, that there are many whose conduct shows they are really enemies of the cross of Christ. They are headed for destruction. Their god is their appetite, they brag about shameful things, and they think only about this life here on earth" (Philippians 3:18-19).

PANDEMIC

Porn's pandemic has spread into our churches. In a 2016 polling of youth pastors and pastors, Barna reported that 57 percent of pastors and 64 percent of youth pastors have struggled with porn. And 5 percent of pastors and 12 percent of youth pastors say they are addicted to it.[3] Churchwide, roughly 50 percent of men and 20 percent of women struggle with pornography. Ninety percent of boys and 60 percent of girls have been exposed to porn before they were 18 years old. This 13-billion-dollar (USA) industry is winning on nearly every front.[4] Couple that with the prevalence of sex addiction (which porn fuels), and you have the greatest human pandemic that is just now being discussed.

CONFESSION

Pornography has been my struggle too. The following painful, shame-laced words are from my memoir, *Thin Places*:

> Early on, my father dulls me to the dangers of pornography. It starts with his penchant for nudity, the way he assumes it to be perfectly normal. In one black and white

picture, I am sitting nude on his friend's lap—a man who is also naked—reading a story. My father asks me to bathe him, to wash his back, to pour water on his head, all while he is stark naked in his claw foot tub. He shows me myriad pictures he takes of unclothed women—some I recognize as his girlfriends, others I don't. I remember one slew of pictures he's particularly proud of: a series of photos where women pose in his bathtub, bubbles surrounding their parts of flesh like the Puget Sound surrounds the San Juan islands. I cringe when he sells some of these black and whites mounted on tag board at his quirky garage sale.

One picture haunts me still.

I am standing outside completely naked next to my terrified friend. I must be nine years old, the age my youngest daughter is now. Making the correlation between her sweet innocence and me back then brings tears to my eyes. I remember when the picture is taken. We are at someone's house near a beach—a wild tangle of grounds that a gaggle of kids try to conquer. We scour the beach. We make faces when the adults say they're making clam spaghetti. And as dusk nears, my friend, another girl my age, and I decide to be naked. Am I the instigator? My father? I doubt it's my friend because I can see the look of horror on her face in the picture my father takes of us.

Old growth evergreens stand behind us. We are skinny and pale in the shrinking light. She wears shock on her face, her eyes wild with shame. She is covering herself up as best as she can, but she has only two hands. The contrast between us is night and day. I wear no such shocked expression. My face is serene, like the Virgin Mary in renaissance paintings. I cover myself because my friend does, but because my father has normalized nudity, I look as if I'm watching the Brady Bunch on TV. Just another day with my father snapping pictures.

That photo captures how I have been groomed to think

it's entirely normal to be nine and naked with my friend. As nine turns to ten, then pre-adolescence turns to adolescence, the rape at five and this normalcy of nudity boils inside me like a witch's brew. And I start an addictive journey. It begins in fifth grade when I follow a group of kids from school to an attic where piles of pornography woo me into a dirty addiction.[5]

I battled that addiction into my teens and early twenties–something I was told women don't face. My friend Jessica Harris has bravely stepped into the arena, chronicling her own battle, and speaks to thousands about women addicted to porn.[6] In my own addiction, I faced a terrible dichotomy in my Christian walk. I knew sex was to be revered and saved—it was a holy act confined to marriage, but in the pictures and prose I read, it was a salacious, self-gratifying act, full of deeper and deeper levels of depravity. I couldn't reconcile the two in my mind, so when I was able to walk away from porn, I shut the door entirely.

This, of course, made seeing the sexual act as beautiful quite difficult. I've been on a journey of learning to reclaim the rightness of sexual expression in marriage (with the additional hurdle of my past sexual abuse), and it has not been easy. In the midst of my fight, I became an advocate for those who have suffered from sexual abuse. And the more I advocated, the more I saw the insidious effects of porn. I'm not saying porn always causes sexual assault. There are many people who have watched or used porn who do not prey on others, just as statistics show that those who have been sexually abused are not doomed to also become predators. People *choose* to assault.

PORN AND ITS AFTEREFFECTS

Porn can produce aberrant thoughts. And with that aberrant thought, some people choose to exploit one another. The question becomes: What influences their choices to violate others? The problem with porn is that it causes many to become completely desensitized to depravity. It exemplifies a sexual act without community, a one-sided, self-centered endeavor, and it's often exploitative on the other side of the screen. People become commodities to be used, not image bearers to cherish.

Many say porn is harmless, but I would assert that any time a man or woman or child or trafficked victim is objectified for their sexual appeal, and that objectification is proliferated, it corrupts minds and creates addiction. In short, people grow tired of simply *seeing* depravity; eventually, some choose to act it out on willing and unwilling "partners." Some delve deeper into porn involving children. We must remember that the porn from many people's childhoods is now entirely different. Advocate Jessica Harris warns:

> In the case of normalized sexual trauma, today's online porn is worlds different from the magazines of the 80s. A majority of pornographic scenes today feature some level of abuse, be that physical or verbal. It conditions the viewer to believe that the behavior they're seeing is not only acceptable, but desired. So, not only is it ok to have rough sex, but a woman secretly enjoys it.[7]

Couple this with the need for more deviance, and you see pornographic imagery growing more and more debased. "Porn users demand a constant stream of new, increasingly violent and fetishized content. In order to keep up with this demand, more women and children become prostituted and trafficked."[8] All this, of course, gets back to money. Porn sells. Porn makes money. People who sell other people in human trafficking make money. Pimps make money. Porn creators make money. And when there is a lot of money to be made, there will be victims who are exploited—those who have no voice. Children, trafficked people, the down and out, the drug-addicted, the runaway, those aging out of the foster system fall prey to an industry that, like a monster with an insatiable appetite, must become more and more depraved to thrive.

And when these kinds of pornographic visuals make their way into someone's mind, they stay there. But not only that, the images and videos normalize aberrant behavior. They cause people to think that everyone welcomes bondage (Hello, *Fifty Shades of Grey*). They preach self-satisfaction to the detriment of the person being objecti-fied. Porn transforms people from the children of a benevolent Cre-ator into impersonal objects to be used for selfish pleasure, all outside the context of relationship. And if that message is received by some-one who already possesses a predatory bent, that person has the poten-tial to become a criminal.

THE PROBLEM

Consider these eye-opening statistics if you don't think there is a problem with porn in our world:

- Porn websites net more traffic than Netflix, Amazon, & Twitter combined.[9]
- Thirty-five percent of all downloaded content is porn-related.[10]
- Child porn is one of the fastest-growing online businesses.[11]
- Over 624,000 child porn traders have been discovered online in the U.S.[12]
- Porn increased marital infidelity by 300 percent.[13]
- At least 30 percent of all data transferred across the Inter-net is porn-related.[14]

And these:

- Every second, 28,258 users are watching pornography.
- Every second, $3,075.64 is being spent on pornography.
- Forty million American people regularly visit porn sites.[15]

PORN AND SEXUAL ABUSE

Sexual abuse occurs when someone deems another person as a dis-pensable object, when he or she believes his or her sexual gratification trumps another person's right to self-determine. Sexual abuse is an act of power and control, often involving violence, threats, and bodily harm. Much of what is watched online exemplifies this kind of objectification exactly.

Having grown up in a highly sexualized environment where my father created pornographic images before the massive proliferation of porn on the Internet, I understand this connection. I know that my father's misdeeds didn't end with images—those images were sometimes acted upon. Because of the connection between images and actions, we need to take a serious look at the insidious, criminally charged nature of pornography. It is a disgrace and an evil blight upon our world. Pornographic images, videos, and words *do* have a negative impact on the minds of those who watch. One can become addicted to porn. Porn can ruin marriages, opening the door to serial infidelity. It can fuel fantasies that sometimes morph into rape realities.

The problem is that porn is everywhere. It lurks in the shadows *and* it brazenly parades in the open. The industry is well-fueled and lucrative. Perhaps there needs to be another movement like MADD (Mothers Against Drunk Driving) called MAPP—Mothers Against Porn Proliferation. Or maybe the church needs to continue to explain the beauty of sex within marriage. Or maybe we need to talk more openly about porn addiction in our pews. I'm not sure of solutions, but I do believe this: Sexual assault is one of the most insidious weapons Satan uses against humanity; porn, likewise, can be a means to that end.

It is high time we become outraged. I think of that little girl standing naked beneath the evergreens, the lack of fright on my face, the way I'd been groomed to believe it was normal to pose without clothes. I shiver to think of what more could have happened to me. And I weep for how many people have been victimized for the sake of another's twisted pleasure. Because of porn's pervasiveness, we're seeing an unprecedented uptick in sex trafficking around the world—an issue that has, thankfully, roused the sleeping church. Since 2007, over 34,000 people have been trafficked in the United States, and one in seven trafficked victims is a runaway. Nearly five million people are being trafficked worldwide.[16] Ministries like the A21 campaign, IJM, ZOE International, and First Aid Arts are working to address the problem, rescue trafficked people, and provide restoration in the aftermath.

Consider this: If there were no need for images of explicit sex—something heavily fueled by the porn industry—there would be no demand for trafficked human beings. Perhaps we've been looking at this issue all wrong, attacking a heinous symptom without rooting out the actual problem. Porn demoralizes others. It is often laced with violence against victims. Porn reinforces the power dynamic of abuser and abused. It normalizes abhorrent behavior. "Study after study has shown that consumers of violent and nonviolent porn are more likely to use verbal coercion, drugs, and alcohol to coerce individuals into sex."[17] Porn also changes the brains of those who watch it. Our "mirror neurons" fire not only when we *do* something sexually exploitive, but also when we *watch* something similar. These mirror neurons are what make us empathetic to a character in a movie. We are sharing their experience as if it's our own. "So if a person feels aroused watching a man or woman get kicked around and called names, that individual's brain learns to associate that kind of violence with sexual arousal."[18] If there were a cheerleader for sexual assault, it would be porn. If there were a rocket fuel for crossing over from watching to performing sexual abuse, it would be porn. If there were a blueprint for sexual exploitation, it would be porn.

There are some who believe porn is a victimless encounter, and that it actually prevents rape because the pornographic image can substitute for acting out. In an online article on the site "Fight the New Drug," this position is exemplified in a tweet: "Also, porn, if anything, *prevents* rape and child molestation. Porn is a sex substitute, not an aphrodisiac."[19] The National Center on Sexual Exploitation (NCOSE) disagrees with this notion, as a lengthy report demonstrates.[20] They reported that "women who were exposed to pornography as children were more likely to accept rape myths and to have sexual fantasies that involved rape."[21] Men who were exposed to mainstream pornography were more likely to entertain the idea of rape, particularly if they could be assured they'd get away with it. Their viewing of porn also caused them to be much less likely to intervene if someone were being raped. Consuming porn also increased the likelihood, both in men and women, of physical and verbal abuse of others. Watching porn has also been correlated with domestic violence and abuse. Di McLeod, Director of the Gold Coast Centre Against Sexual Violence (Australia), writes the following: "What research is finding and what we are seeing at our centre is that pornography is clearly influencing sexual expectations and practices between intimate partners, so that the correlation between pornography, rape, and domestic violence can no longer be ignored."[22]

Dr. Robert Jensen of the University of Texas found this correlation between male use of pornography and what they believe constitutes consensual sex:

> My own studies and reviews of other examinations of content suggest there are a few basic themes in pornography: (1) All women at all times want sex from all men, (2) women enjoy all the sexual acts that men perform or demand, and, (3) any woman who does not at first realize this can be easily turned with a little force, though force is rarely necessary because most of the women in pornography are the imagined nymphomaniacs about whom many men fantasize.[23]

With the proliferation of campus date rape, one can see clearly how a warped view of sex, exacerbated by porn and alcohol, accounts for its steep ascent.

THE INFILTRATION OF THE CHURCH

Perhaps this is why so few in the church come to the aid of sexual abuse survivors. Perhaps the shame associated with their own porn-in-the-pocket use has desensitized those who would have been protectors. Perhaps the secrecy of church leaders' addictions has dulled them to the very real cry of survivors. Advocate Jessica Harris explains,

> Pornography is setting up to be the largest issue in the church. While current leadership may have less of a problem, the younger generations are saturated in it. One

church reached out to me because 100% of their teen girls were struggling with pornography. I was speaking at a church a couple years ago and a twelve-year-old went to her friend's mom and said, 'I don't see what the big deal is, every girl watches porn.' This issue is far more prevalent in churches than most of us in ministry realize. I have gotten to the point when I speak that I assume, unless it's an older crowd, 50-75% of the people I'm speaking to struggle with pornography.[24]

Can you see Satan's strategy here? Get a lot of people, starting when they're children, addicted to pornography—if they go to church or lead the church, all the better. Desensitize them to the plight of survivors. Keep them enslaved and secretive. While some keep their addictions secret, others act out, perpetrating harm against others. But so few will intervene because of the shame of it all. This is how human souls can become deeply entrenched in sexual aberrance. If survivors are simply part of a rape fantasy, if they secretly want to be abused, and Christian leaders are watching (and neural mirroring) these deplorable actions, then exposing sexual abuse hits awfully close to home. To expose another is to welcome possible introspection into your own addiction. Best to keep it all quiet.

Who suffers in this scenario? Certainly the abused—because they are not heard, and few people intervene on their behalf. But the porn-addicted suffer too, because of their enslaved state. It is time for light—a holy shining on the darkness that has proliferated and infiltrated our churches like the worst form of cancer. The church is ineffective because many who name the name of Jesus are chasing the idol of pornography.

I would be remiss if I didn't say there is hope for the enslaved. Paul finishes his warning in Philippians with a potent reminder: "We are citizens of heaven, where the Lord Jesus Christ lives. And we are eagerly waiting for him to return as our Savior. He will take our weak mortal bodies and change them into glorious bodies like his own, using the same power with which he will bring everything under his control" (3:20-21). Jesus is always the answer to our cravings—not our ability to follow him, but his ability to redeem us. When we admit our weakness, his strength has a chance to shine. When we let him into those scarred places, he has a chance to shine. And when we dare to admit our addiction to others in the body of Christ, we give permission for others to do likewise. Light breeds light. Freedom inaugurates more freedom. Truth begets truth.

As I've written elsewhere, this "reminds me of the cure for idolatry that Timothy Keller writes about in his book *Counterfeit Gods*. We can't simply forsake our idols (whether they be materialism, achievement, lust, the desire to please, food, porn, reputation, or anything else). Instead, we must worship that which is higher. Repentance must hold hands with rejoicing. That's how life pushes out the dead leaves in our lives. We rejoice. We embrace the Life Giver and praise His worth. And His life, because of its sheer power and beauty, pushes away death."[25]

We have settled for much less, chasing our appetites while forsaking the only One who can satiate our innate hunger. Oh, dear church, chase the One who satisfies, who is our life indeed, letting go of the darkness beneath.

CHAPTER SEVEN

THE PROBLEM OF PREDATORS

*[Larry Nassar] was up early and went to bed late.
He would do anything for an injured athlete.
He was an astonishingly giving person.*[1]

We have it all wrong. We picture predatory people, particularly sexual abusers, as creeps driving windowless vans through neighborhoods, trolling for children. We view them as outcasts, socially awkward, incredibly easy to spot. Sadly, we trust more in our instinct to uncover this kind of predator than in an *actual* predator's grand ability to deceive. While people who fulfill this van stereotype exist, the vast majority of serial sexual predators lead astonishingly normal lives—at least in one sphere. It is in the other hidden part where they've mastered their deception. They are coaches, teachers, community activists, clergy—seemingly upstanding citizens and unfailingly generous. They are your neighbors, friends, and leaders. Their ability to appear normal or even amazing is their effective cover. This is why they get away with harming so many. When their two lives collide, the friends and family members of the abuser often choose not to believe his or her predation to be true. *He's such a nice man. She's such a giving person. How could it be true?*

TRAITS

It's imperative we learn to discern the nature of predatory people, understanding how they operate and what traits they exhibit. In my book *The Seven Deadly Friendships,* I listed characteristics of a personality I dubbed "Predator Paige." Here are a few of her traits:

- She seems too perfect. She seems to have everything together.

- She is admirable, the kind of person you'd want to emulate.

- She hides her sociopathic tendencies by creating admirable facades that fit nicely into each situation.

- She tends to distract you easily from her faults, making others out to be the reason she has even tiny faults (it's all someone else's fault).

- She easily morphs into what you admire.

- Her daily currency is deceit. She cannot tell the truth or discern it.[2]

- She is never, ever wrong. Predatory people will go to any length to avoid personal responsibility. Besides blaming the survivor (see above), she cannot exist in a world where she has flaws or perceived sins. So she deflects. She makes anyone who brings up her actions into a heinous, callous villain.

- She has elaborate conspiracy theories about people out to get her in order to deflect the true things those people or groups of people have against her. She always has a carefully prepared explanation and excuse for getting caught.[3]

Sexual predators spend a lifetime perfecting their techniques. Theirs is not a crime of convenience (where a victim just happened to come across their path), but of continual, dogged, meticulous preparation. They study. Like a velociraptor, they learn. And try new techniques constantly. Like magicians, they have the uncanny ability to achieve sleight of hand—even in front of parents or bystanders. A perpetrator considers perfecting predatory methods as their number one full-time occupation. They spend hours upon hours honing their skills, testing boundaries.

Sexual predators are often charming. They get away with serial predation precisely because they've honed their interpersonal skills and practiced how to put people at ease. They know how to befriend and be kind to 98 percent of the population—and at the same time seek out the vulnerable. They tell the vulnerable 2 percent that no one would believe even if they did tell. Why? Because, as I mentioned above, they are typically not people you'd expect to be predatory. The 98 percent is part of their overall plan. In 98 percent of their lives, they're upstanding, helpful, generous, funny, self-deprecating, "honest," and engaging. So if or when survivors bring something to light, very few believe them. Why? Because who wants to believe that your amazing friend is actually a wolf in sheep's clothing? Surely not! Surely the #MeToo movement has gone crazy if it can even accuse this wonderful person of such a heinous crime. Knowing just how hard it was for me to disclose my own abuse, I know that the grand majority of people who quietly whisper their abuse are telling the truth.

Predatory people spin stories. They have learned how to demean and demoralize a victim to such an extent that after you read or hear their words, you're convinced the predator is the victim. Be very cautious about a predatory person who plays on your empathy. Be hypervigilant when a person demeans their accusers or gossips maliciously about anyone who has brought an accusation to light. They also tend to say convincing words about nefarious acts of sexual abuse. Jimmy Hinton's clergy father, who admitted to abusing 23 children, certainly fits this description. Jimmy said the following:

> "I didn't know that an average abuser (of children) usually has 150 victims by the time they get caught, if they ever get caught. I don't think they have much regard for human life. When you can do that to a child and leave them crying and begging you to stop, but you do it anyway, you have no

regard for human life. The words are there though," he said. He heard his father during several sermons preach that children must be protected from being sexually abused. He called such acts "the worst evil in the world."[4]

Some repent, but only superficially, and *only* after they've been truly exposed. While genuine repentance can sometimes happen after someone is caught in the act (see Matthew 18, or the man caught with his father's wife in 1 Corinthians 5 and 2 Corinthians 2), if a predatory person repents *only after exposure*, be cautious. There's a vast difference between saying eloquent words of repentance after being caught and actually quietly repenting, asking forgiveness of each survivor, and working toward restorative justice. And if the repentance language is couched in vagaries like, "I'm sorry so-and-so misinterpreted my actions," or "I may have crossed an ethical boundary, but so did the survivor; this was consensual," be even more wary. True repentance is obvious when it happens. You don't leave a conversation with a truly repentant person second-guessing yourself—you know the person's sorrow and regret. Genuine repentance is always specific and is followed by a remorseful apology and acts of restoration. The one who truly repents cares nothing for their reputation. There is no saving face or salvaging their reputation. Instead, like King David in the Bathsheba narratives, they know they've violated the law of God and are willing to suffer the righteous consequences of their lawless actions. They do not blame. They do not spin. If they could heap dust and ashes upon themselves, they would gladly do it.

Predatory people almost never repent. Why is this? The answer requires us to go back to the narrative in Romans 1 where Paul warns us about the pathway people take when they constantly and consistently shake a fist at God and walk in their own way, satisfying their lusts. "Since they thought it foolish to acknowledge God, he abandoned them to their foolish thinking and let them do things that should never be done" (Romans 1:28). When people have been given over by God, they cannot help but constantly violate his commandments, sinking into deeper levels of depravity. At first this seems innocuous. Predators, because they typically get away with their behavior for years (and some are never caught), become emboldened. If they first touch a leg without consequences, they might push more physical boundaries. While they begin their abuse in private, eventually they'll begin perpetrating these acts in front of others—just for the thrill of it. For years, they are creeks, flowing into new places of predation, not realizing that each day, each month, each act is carving their behavior into a ditch, then a trench, then a canyon. And once their actions have taken them into the bowels of Grand Canyon–like depths, it is nearly impossible to climb out. The longer the abhorrent behavior, the steeper the journey back to normalcy.

WHY DO THEY SUCCEED?

The Catholic Church issued a report about the causes of their own clergy abuse, much to many people's outrage. The lion's share of the blame is directed at society, and the sexual revolution of the 1960s: "The report theorizes that priests coming of age in the 1940s and 1950s, growing up in families where sexuality was a taboo topic, and trained in seminaries that did not prepare them for lives of celibacy, went on to violate children during the social chaos of the sexual revolution."[5] They also believed the clergy sexual abuse crisis has passed, peaking in the mid 1980s—something statistics and the #MeToo movement are constantly challenging. So why do sexual predators prey on victims? Should we blame the 1960s? No.

They prey because they can. Usually a perpetrator has authority (older, a church leader, a parent, an adult) over the victim and can use intimidation to keep them silent. He may tell a child that he will kill his or her parents, or make up other horrifying reasons why the child must not tell. Because of their authority and because they are often stronger than their prey, the child complies.

They continue to abuse because we live in a culture of silence. My babysitter chose to look the other way. Church leaders prefer reputation over justice, so they cover it up, heaping shame upon shame on the survivor, favoring the predator to the one preyed upon. In this petri dish of silence, where no one is brought to task or judgment, abusers flourish and reproduce.

Some predators cannot meet their emotional needs in normal relationships. Because of familial dysfunction, detachment issues, or their own sexual trauma, they've learned the only way to get close to someone is to dominate and humiliate and coerce. They falsely believe this constitutes a personal relationship, and this need must be met continually through further victimization.

They become intoxicated by getting away with their crime. One study in 1992 showed that only 12 percent of rapes in the United States were reported. A later study found that number to be 32 percent. "The low rate of reporting leads to the conclusion that the approximate 265,000 convicted sex offenders under the authority of corrections agencies in the United States (Greenfeld, 1997) represent less than 10% of all sex offenders living in communities nationwide."[6] The implication, therefore, is that 90 percent of sex offenders live in the free world, getting away with their predation. Each subsequent victim fuels a sexual abuser's sense of invincibility and his or her need to continue. After all, typically they will not be caught.

Why do sexual predators get away with their actions?

- Some get away with it because of self-deception and their cunning ability to convince others of their stellar public persona. They do this through an elaborate facade or excessively charming words.

- Many truly believe that what they're doing is *not* wrong. They've minimized their actions as something trivial, and therefore feel no remorse. So there are no "tells" of their abuse. No remorse. No guilt. They have the capability to feign normalcy because they truly believe they *are* normal.

- Some predatory people rationalize their behavior, actually believing that what they do benefits the survivor. This ties into the above reason. If they're happy and proud of their actions, they won't agonize.

- Because the perpetrator has dehumanized their victims, they've reduced their prey to a vehicle for their pleasure. This dehumanization often results from violating their consciences over and over again until they believe those they abuse "deserve" it. This self-righteous belief is something they don't share publicly. They realize sharing this view would incur shock and possible prosecution, so they playact their "normal citizen" role.

You'll notice that few of these getting-away-with-it reasons has to do with culture or society—it's sin and deviation lurking within the perpetrator that compels them, coupled with a hefty dose of evil. While our highly sexualized culture contributes greatly to the problem, the true issue is the heart. All abusive behavior flows from a hard heart, from one choice that leads to many, many choices until the conscience is seared and no longer in operation. Abuse thrives when we are silent, like the cover-ups in clergy abuse scandals. It thrives under cronyism, where a system must be preserved at any cost, even if that cost means survivors are ignored, silenced, or ridiculed.

SCRIPTURAL UNDERSTANDING

We must remember what the Bible teaches as we think about sexual predators, particularly those who attend church:

> These people are false apostles. They are deceitful workers who disguise themselves as apostles of Christ. But I am not surprised! Even Satan disguises himself as an angel of light. So it is no wonder that his servants also disguise themselves as servants of righteousness. In the end they will get the punishment their wicked deeds deserve (2 Corinthians 11:13-15).

Those in pastoral leadership who abuse their congregants may appear to be holy, but they will be found out (and we are seeing a massive cleaning of house these days!). No wolf in sheep's clothing can pull the wool over the eyes of the almighty, all-knowing God.

These perpetrators get away with their crimes for so long because they're adept at manipulation and deception. But they also get away with it because we don't want to live in a world where clergy hurt people, so we afford them the benefit of the doubt way more than we do survivors. If we believe survivors, it plunges us into a chaotic world in which those we thought would protect, prey instead. And that is frightening. Better to keep up the ruse for the status quo. I see this in the town I live in, where people simply don't want to believe that seemingly good, upstanding citizens prey on others.

Predators reflect their true allegiance, which is to the father of lies, who came explicitly to ruin humanity. I can think of no other crime, other than murder, that leaves a human more damaged and broken than sexual abuse. Its long-lasting trauma causes survivors to question the goodness of God. Abuse fuels depressive thoughts, even suicidal ideation. It seeps into every relationship, particularly romantic ones. Many survivors I've interacted with can no longer have sex because of flashbacks, triggers, and an overall equating of sex with abuse. The trauma from abuse affects health, which then influences economic viability. Internal strife, external relational damage, livelihood—all are negatively influenced by sexual assault.

Still, Jesus didn't leave us without resources. Consider his warning: "Behold, I am sending you out as sheep in the midst of wolves, so be wise as serpents and innocent as doves" (Matthew 10:16 ESV). We live in a world of wool-wearing wolves. We must be wise. We must uncover the deceptive practices of sexual abusers. Educating yourself about this and exposing the darkness is spiritual warfare. Don't back down: Exposing darkness with light is God's handiwork. Remember this, too: "The reason the Son of God appeared was to destroy the works of the devil" (1 John 3:8 ESV). Instead of vilifying whistle-blowers and dismissing survivors, our work is to partner with Christ to expose predatory darkness. We are to "take no part in the worthless deeds of evil and darkness; instead, expose them" (Ephesians 5:11).

WHAT ABOUT REDEMPTION?

In this chapter, we've uncovered the modus operandi of serial abusers. We have discussed the nature of constant predation and the rarity of genuine repentance. But let's say the predatory person actually *has* repented. Shouldn't we offer grace immediately? Are we not people of redemption? Who are we to cast stones? Wouldn't we be better off looking at our own sin? Is it not gossip to even talk about today's sexual abuse scandals?

It is not gossip to expose predators. It's telling the truth for the sake of preventing future victims. When they began harming others, they relinquished their right to privacy. And in terms of casting stones, yes, of course we examine ourselves. But what if our introspection means we fail to report predation? What if society operated that way? What if I knew that a person was a murderer and would most likely murder again? Would I refrain from reporting simply because I, too, struggle with sin? How ridiculous is that? My own sin struggle is a separate issue from the responsibility of being an agent of justice. My greater allegiance must be to the One who made us, who calls murder (and rape) wrong. My allegiance must be to protect the innocent—following the footsteps of my Savior who did the same.

My friend Jennifer put it this way:

> Forgiveness—biblical or otherwise—never entails the dismissal or denial of consequences. Quite the opposite, in fact. This carte blanche, faux grace is as insidious as it is heretical. Grace is never to be a cloak for vice, and true repentance—the real, original word—involves turning and going the other way. There shouldn't be any trumpeting of the perpetrators' newfound victimhood or hiding behind some kind of childish squeal of "Can't touch me, I'm safe because I said the Magic Words!" The response of these folks is garbage. Fear-fueled, people-pleasing, ear-tickling garbage.[7]

Redemption is more nuanced than blindly conferring it upon perpetrators. First, if the predator is not genuinely repentant, offering them quick, cheap grace simply emboldens and empowers them to continue unchecked in their predatory behavior. *Do we really want that to happen?* And if the predatory person has abused their power, it would be unkind to them and to future victims to welcome them back into their arena of temptation. However, so many stories all over the world and throughout Christendom favor the narrative of redemption, even to the detriment of further victims. Abusers are allowed to do the predatory shuffle—to move from publishing house, to position of authority, to speaker, to luminary. This makes it even harder for survivors to speak up. The fame and believability of the one in power overshadows the "small" story of the abused.

Let's not forget that this is *not* about sex. This is *not* about consensual affairs. This is about coercive control and abuse of power. Even so, let's say the person has truly repented (more than just feeling bad about being exposed, but a genuine horror at the damage they've done to others). Even if he or she repents and asks for forgiveness and goes to therapy to understand personal deviance (which is an important part of the eventual restoration process), their actions don't negate two very important facts:

1. Ethical standards have been violated (and, in many instances, crime has occurred).

2. The survivor remains harmed, and is left to deal with the aftermath of the abuser's actions.

HIT AND RUN

Imagine an unruly drunk driver. Perhaps he's been caught in smaller indiscretions before, been warned many times, or maybe he's gotten away with it for years. Even so, on one particular day, this drunk driver jumps a curb and hits an unsuspecting pedestrian. (And it doesn't matter what that pedestrian was wearing.) He flees.

The driver begins to believe that there are no repercussions for driving drunk. So he keeps doing it, continuing to jump curbs and harm people—people who have to go to the hospital, who enter rehab to learn how to walk again, who will never be the same. But for the driver, there's no repentance. No getting caught. Just more drunken driving, more harm, more brazen confidence—all while he publicly excels in other areas, seemingly unaffected by what he's done. He even compensates for his behavior by joining a support group for survivors of drunk drivers and makes speeches about the evils of driving while intoxicated. Because of this, he's the last person you'd expect to be a serial offender.

Then one day, the investigator on all these cases uncovers camera footage for every accident, and the authorities arrest him. The drunk driver, faced with incriminating evidence over the span of years, confesses, then "repents." Even so, he cannot take back the harm. The hit and runs happened (many times, many lives). All that criminal activity devastated the pedestrians who now battle injuries for life, whether or not the driver repented. The man's "repentance" cannot negate the crime, nor can it erase the damage done. In order to move on with their lives without bitterness, the survivors may have forgiven him, but even that forgiveness does not erase the crime committed.

The drunk driver will be prosecuted, and if he ever gets out of prison, he'll most likely not be allowed to operate a car again, or he'll have to breathe into a device to be able to start his car. And the survivors will have the right to file civil cases against the driver to be recompensed financially for all the pain, medical care, and damages done to them.

Now imagine that the drunk driver is a sexual predator. Sadly, in the case of sexual assault or harassment, survivors seldom sue, and these situations seldom darken the courtroom. But the analogy stands. Even if the perpetrator repents, that does not make everything happy again, tied up in a bow.

So let's tread carefully. We must be discerning when someone (who has multiple victims) claims to repent. Just because the person is nice or seems sad, remember that there are people aching in the aftermath of their predation, and that even the perpetrator's repentance cannot remove what has already been done. "We are all sinners," people say when a sexual predator who happens to be a Christian leader is outed. Some other frustrating responses:

- "Let's not cast the first stone."
- "Gossip is a sin, so by posting or warning, you are gossiping."
- "Judge not lest you be judged."
- "Women should expect harassment and get over it. They're being too sensitive, weak."
- "We need to be people of grace."

Yes, of course, we are all sinners. But not all of us are criminals. Not all of us break laws and prey on the vulnerable. Not all of us stalk our victims. There is a vast legal difference between someone who has sinned and someone who committed a crime or multiple crimes. Remember, sin separates us from a holy God, but crime separates us from law-abiding society. In other words, while all crime is sin, not all sin is crime. We can offer grace to our brothers and sisters who commit crimes, but that grace is best given in the context of justice being administered by the appropriate authorities, when they are behind bars.

But what about our tightly (and rightly) held views that a supposed perpetrator is innocent until proven guilty? Yes, this is true, but remember that sexual assault is difficult to prosecute, and that few people report their crimes. And if they do, they face a deluge of victim-blaming, questioning, and an onslaught of online abuse. The question becomes: Do we need a jury's final verdict to determine whether evil has occurred? In our criminal justice system, there are many instances where the statute of limitations prevents a trial in the first place. Or there are crimes committed by criminals that never see prosecution. Does this make a murderer innocent of murder?[8]

People who naively respond with "grace, grace," which I would argue is cheapened by our nonchalant use of it, simply do not understand the nature of a predatory person—something we've discussed at length in this chapter. Hear me: You can absolutely meet a charming, witty, selfless predator. He or she can woo you to the point that you would trust him or her implicitly. That's how predation works. You could even swear upon a stack of Bibles that this person is utterly innocent because he or she has never, *ever* preyed on you. You never experienced weird vibes around the person, never heard them say raunchy things. In fact, they were the exact opposite of that. Some predators even hide within organizations that try to out predators! They are clever, deceiving, and really, really good at creating a shiny public persona.

The result is that when a survivor (or a group of survivors) levels accusations against a predatory person, it is more likely that people respond with incredulity. They don't want to believe that this amazing person did that awful thing. To think that would be to admit that insidious evil exists in our backyard, our church, our hometown. It would mean that we were bamboozled and fooled by a clever predator. It would put us on shaky ground. Who wants to live in a world in which a youth pastor could do that awful thing? Or a world in which that missionary school could allow so many children to be hurt? Who wants to live in a world in which that celebrity pastor preyed on the women in his office?

We must remember that Satan, the enemy of us all, does not prowl around as a wolf. He dons the sheep's gentle coat, slips in quietly among the fold, then murders in the margins. This is the same practice of a predatory person. He or she will look innocent, lamblike. This nonthreatening, crafted persona of an upstanding human being allows them to slip through the sheepfold—often churches—unnoticed. Why? Because we are so trusting.

People who break the law and harm others do not need our grace or our cries that we're all sinners. And when we say these things to survivors, we revictimize them. For the sake of the innocents harmed and those who are potential victims, predatory people need justice—for their sake so they can no longer harm, and for ours so our families and children are safe.

I mentioned Jimmy Hinton in the introductory chapter—a man who, along with his mother, turned in his father to the police. His father was a serial sexual abuser who molested dozens of girls. As a pastor, Jimmy's father did amazing ministry, performing weddings, visiting the sick, and leading people to Christ. He endeared himself to his church and his community. His "trustworthiness" helped him conceal the predatory portion of his life. Jimmy writes, "My dad has dozens of victims who all have heart-shattering stories of shame, pain, and humiliation. He was able to gain access to children *precisely because* everybody trusted him." You can imagine how horrifically hard it was for the congregation left behind to wrap their minds and hearts around this terrible truth: This pastor they'd known, loved, and revered, was actually a criminal. Jimmy told me, "The first year after his arrest, people would ask me how my dad was doing. Only one person asked me how his victims were doing. Several people said, 'Isn't it a shame that your dad fell into temptation in the past few months?'"[9]

What should have been said—but was not—is this: "Isn't it a shame that we didn't expose him earlier? Isn't it a shame that he had so many victims whose lives will never be the same? Isn't it a shame that this supposed man of God tarnished the reputation of the church by his actions?" That's the shame. In the well-known story of the emperor's new clothes, the reader sees the obvious. Here's this leader walking down the street naked, yet because of social propriety and peer pressure, no one wants to address the obvious. Instead, people feign admiration for the man's "clothes" while he waves at the crowd. It is only when a child proclaims the truth, something along the lines of "Hey, that old guy isn't wearing any clothes," that the crowd suddenly acknowledges the truth. This is the power of the #MeToo movement. Survivors are finding their voices, choosing to tamp down their tangible fear of their perpetrators to state the underlying fact: *This person who seems so amazing is a predator.*

It's time we tell the truth about the naked "emperors" in our midst—for the sake of protecting those who are harmed. It's time we separate sin from crime and call out the reality of the offense—no matter how "good" the perpetrator appears on the outside. We ignore the poison within and the veiled actions without to our peril.

POOP BROWNIES

Predatory people have a dark secret, but they present themselves as innocuous or even welcoming. Imagine a pan of freshly baked brownies made from butter, sugar, eggs, cocoa, vanilla, flour, and one surprising ingredient: 2 percent human excrement. If you were ignorant of the last ingredient, you'd be grabbing a tub of ice cream and à la moding the chocolate treat. But if you knew? You'd quickly discard the entire dish. Like tainted treats, predators possess an "unsavory" side, to put it mildly. Upon examination, and because only 2 percent of the brownies contain feces, they smell like brownies too. This is why they slip into churches undetected. Placed alongside non-poop brownies, they would look identical. *But they are not the same.* That 2 percent absolutely matters. It has been inexorably mixed in with the rest of the batter. It permeates the brownies. Never mind that most of the confection is good. The 2 percent negates the 98 percent. And those brownies have infected and forever tainted survivors who will never be the same. We err so often by offering grace to the perpetrators, while leveling harsh judgment on the survivors who dare to stand up and swear to the 2 percent.

Every person on this planet sins. But not all of us create elaborate facades *in order to* prey on people. Not all of us are poop brownies, with devastated survivors in their confectionary wake. Let's call them what they are and expose them. And let's dare to offer survivors the dignity of belief. This is our Christian duty, the church's mandate—to protect the innocent and become a haven for those who are harmed.

The Lord will ultimately prevail over this deception. He already knows the hearts and actions of those who hide behind words and facades. In Isaiah 28:17, God warns: "I will test you with the measuring line of justice and the plumb line of righteousness. Since your refuge is made of lies, a hailstorm will knock it down. Since it is made of deception, a flood will sweep it away." When we no longer hide, when we educate ourselves on the nature of predatory people, when we agree that the world we live in is permeated by evil, then we will act alongside the God of justice, exposing lies, uncovering deception, reporting abuse to the authorities equipped to handle crime, and participating wholly in the restorative process. As the hands, feet, and heart of Jesus, we must act.

CHAPTER EIGHT

THE PASSIVITY OF THE CHURCH

*Christian responses that minimize the evil of abuse
have in turn minimized the righteousness of God.*

RACHAEL DENHOLLANDER[1]

Brett Sengstock was seven years old when a celebrity pastor stayed at his parents' home. Every night while there, the pastor would creep into Brett's bedroom and molest him. Brett recalled, "I could not speak. I couldn't scream. I couldn't push back. I just went rigid, and I couldn't breathe. I was petrified."[2]

Later, the head of the Assemblies of God denomination in Australia told Brett, "You're my golden boy. You're special to me." He perpetuated the abuse until Brett was 12 years old. Brett kept the secret four more years and then told his mom what had happened.

"She turned around, and then said to me, 'You don't want to send people to hell, and stop sending them to the church.'" As you can imagine, Brett kept it quiet for many years.

When Brett was 36, his mom made a choice to let the church know what had happened. The result? The church handled the situation behind the scenes. The man did admit the abuse to church leadership. Then he gave Brett a large sum of money, but without an apology. The perpetrator's son, himself a leader, chose not to report the abuse to the authorities. Bob Cotton, a leader during the time when the crimes

were swept under the rug, began investigating the extent of the predation after reading the stories uncovered by the Royal Commission into
Institutional Responses to Child Sexual Abuse. "Our executive knew
what [he] had done, yet did nothing to protect the innocent and did
everything to protect the assets and cash of the institution and the reputation of [him]."[3]

THE CHURCH'S TYPICAL RESPONSE: PASSIVITY

Tragically, the church's typical response to abuse in its midst has
been passivity. In the case of a youth pastor who allegedly assaulted
one of his students and one megachurch leader accused by multiple
women of sexual harassment, the first response by leaders in authority
is denial, then survivor shaming and blaming. This is followed by the
church's response above—treating the matter as a public relations issue
and attempting to protect their reputation, not a call to the authorities.
The less said and revealed, the less the authorities are involved, the better. If further allegations arise (and they usually do), the church or ministry then typically releases a flurry of statements finally acknowledging
the abuse, but the damage to survivors has already been done, and the
church's reputation, ironically, has already been irreparably damaged.

This type of response leads to secondary trauma for survivors of
sexual assault. To finally share publicly only to be disbelieved and then
maligned means immeasurable pain. Some survivors even believe that
the response to their story is even more traumatic than the assault itself.
No apology in the aftermath can undo the damage done to the survivor—damage that has been enacted publicly. But even behind closed
doors, such a response to abuse can be devastating. One survivor of
priestly sexual abuse in Northern Ireland, Sean Faloon, met with a nun
half a dozen times where he disclosed his abuse. Eventually, the nun
replied, "Given time, God will forgive you." Sean said, "It stayed with
me, and angers me and my family to this day what she said."[4]

I have to ask the simple question: What would Jesus do? Is this
how he would treat the broken and downtrodden? With public shaming and humiliation or private blame? Is this how he would deal with

sexual abuse allegations? Knowing that Jesus reserved his harshest words for those in religious authority who abused their followers, he would also speak truth to power in these situations. After all, sexual abuse within the church is a terrible blight, a detestably sad reality, an irrevocable scar.

Jesus warned leaders who preferred reputation to truth…and his words remain relevant in our own era: "Everything they do is for show. On their arms they wear extra wide prayer boxes with Scripture verses inside, and they wear robes with extra long tassels. And they love to sit at the head table at banquets and in the seats of honor in the synagogues. They love to receive respectful greetings as they walk in the marketplaces, and to be called 'Rabbi'" (Matthew 23:5-7). Simply put, leaders who love the limelight are in danger of treating survivors with contempt. Jesus later continues, "What sorrow awaits you teachers of religious law and you Pharisees. Hypocrites! For you are so careful to clean the outside of the cup and the dish, but inside you are filthy—full of greed and self-indulgence! You blind Pharisee! First wash the inside of the cup and the dish, and then the outside will become clean, too" (Matthew 23:25-26). Note that the Pharisees were beset with the twin sins of greed and self-indulgence. How many sexual abuse scandals within the church would have been handled properly had the leadership let go of their greed? How many scandals would have been avoided in the first place had the predator forsook self-indulgence?

There is a crisis of leadership in today's evangelical church. It may be easy to point the finger at the Roman Catholic Church for their errant handling of sexual abuse cases, shuffling predators from one church to another and giving them access to more and more victims, but consider this: Don't we do the same? Protestant churches have no internal or interdenominational system of reporting or even warning others. The left hand often has no idea what the right hand is doing. This was the case for one survivor, who was assaulted by her youth pastor when she was a minor. When she reported the abuse ten years later to the International Mission Board (the mission entity of the Southern Baptist Convention, SBC), they investigated the accusation and found the survivor's claims credible, and the accused chose to step down.[5] However, the man continued ministering in SBC churches and eventually became the Chief Strategist of the South Carolina Baptist Convention in 2016. In 2018, after learning of his position and working through her very real trauma, the survivor reported him to the Fort Worth, Texas, authorities. David Platt, former head of the IMB (International Mission Board), apologized to her in a public statement: "I want to publicly apologize for the hurt and pain that [she] has specifically suffered in this situation." He thanked her for "the courage she showed in approaching IMB in 2007, and the courage she is showing now."[6]

This is a worldwide problem. The uncovering of cover-ups is happening everywhere. As I write, 3,677 sexual abuse cases in Germany have been reported in the Roman Catholic Church, with half of the survivors being under the age of 13.[7] French bishops have vowed to look into the issue.[8] In 2015, the Mennonite Church USA conducted a service of lament in response to serious allegations against the late theologian John Howard Yoder, who preyed on his female students.[9]

In an interview with *The Christian Century*, Boz Tchividjian highlighted the problem of the evangelical church's response to the current sexual abuse scandals:

> Evangelicals often frown upon transparency and accountability as many Protestants rely on scripture more than religious leaders, compared to Catholics. Abusers condemn gossip in their efforts to keep people from reporting abuse. Survivors are also admonished to protect the reputation of Jesus. Too many Protestant institutions have sacrificed souls in order to protect their institutions. We've got the Gospels backwards.[10]

#METOO

For those marginalized by the institutional church's response, we must understand that the movement that started authentic revelations of sexual abuse is on a meteoric rise. In 2006, Tarana Burke coined "Me Too" to empower women to share their stories of sexual assault and find camaraderie among other survivors. She planted a seed for an explosion 11 years later. On October 5, 2017, actress Ashley Judd publicly outed Harvey Weinstein in a story for the *New York Times*—detailing his sexually abusive behavior. Ten days later, Alyssa Milano tweeted, "If you've been sexually harassed or assaulted write 'me too' as a reply to this tweet." The response? Beyond belief, producing a worldwide movement of survivors sharing their stories, often publicly for the first time. From this movement, many began to "fall."

From this movement, many began to fall—physicians, coaches, actors, directors, senators, TV hosts, comedians, radio personalities, celebrity and noncelebrity chefs, conductors, CEOs, singers, and political nominees.

The church has also faced its #MeToo reckoning with the abovementioned scandals involving pastors and denominational leaders. The former president of Southwestern Theological Seminary stunned many with his insensitive remarks when he encouraged a woman in his congregation to endure domestic violence, in addition to choosing to "break down" a rape victim during his stint at Southeastern Baptist Theological Seminary.[11] A writing professor, author, and sought-after speaker at Christian writing conferences faced many allegations of sexual harassment spanning decades. The chief doctor at a mission hospital in Bangladesh sexually assaulted dozens of children in his care—all unchecked.

A SAD CASE STUDY

We see a microcosm of the problem with a case that preceded the #MeToo movement when a popular family-based reality show faced its own crisis. One of the family's sons molested his sisters and a babysitter. The evangelical response further shows just how broken and uninformed we are. A well-known politician wrote this on his Facebook page:

> The reason that the law protects disclosure of many actions on the part of a minor is that the society has traditionally understood something that today's blood-thirsty media

does not understand—that being a minor means that one's judgement [sic] is not mature. No one needs to defend [his] actions as a teenager, but the fact that he confessed his sins to those he harmed, sought help, and has gone forward to live a responsible and circumspect life as an adult is testament to his family's authenticity and humility.[12]

What this boy did was not only a sin to be repented of; it was a crime according to the state he resided in—a punishable crime with lasting repercussions, not only for him (had he been convicted prior to the statute of limitations, he would have been registered as a sex offender) but also for his survivors who will spend a lifetime healing. Anyone who knew of this crime and did not report it also could be considered guilty of breaking the law. Teachers, among other professionals, are mandatory reporters. They are required to report abuse to the authorities if they become aware of it. Since this family homeschooled their children, one could make the argument that as home educators, they would be required to report the sexual abuse right away to the proper authorities, not simply to a church or board of elders.

Why? Because, again, what their son did was a crime, not a teenage indiscretion or experiment. And whether he repented or not is not the issue. Yes, we can offer him grace. We can walk alongside and support. But grace does not negate the legal consequences of criminal acts. The Bible is even clear about what we should do if we see evil and do nothing about it: "Remember, it is sin to know what you ought to do and then not do it" (James 4:17).

Scripture welcomes civil authorities and government entities to bring criminals to justice: "The authorities are God's servants, sent for your good. But if you are doing wrong, of course you should be afraid, for they have the power to punish you. They are God's servants, sent for the very purpose of punishing those who do what is wrong. So you must submit to them, not only to avoid punishment, but also to keep a clear conscience" (Romans 13:4-5). You yourself understand the importance of a just and civil government, one that acts on behalf of the welfare of its people.

All this would seem to be a moot point because the boy's crime did not get reported in a timely enough manner to have the judicial system render a verdict. However, a greater issue, at present, is this: justice. Ultimately, where is the justice—not for the perpetrator, not for the reputation of his famous parents, but for the survivors of his criminal acts? It is clear that God stands on the side of the survivor, and he asks all of us to be similar agents of restoration and reconciliation. Throughout Scripture we are encouraged: "Learn to do good. Seek justice. Help the oppressed. Defend the cause of orphans. Fight for the rights of widows" (Isaiah 1:17). As I mentioned earlier in this book, both orphans and widows represented the voiceless and defenseless of society—an apt description for a little girl who slept and awoke to a teenage boy touching her in inappropriate ways.

I find it deeply saddening that this perpetrator's victims seem to be forgotten in this discussion. They never asked to be violated or forcibly fondled. They were the unwitting recipients of his choice to sexually abuse them. He made the choice. He violated their bodies and their trust. Yet he gets all the mercy while survivors become an inconvenient footnote? How does that represent the God who stands on the side of the marginalized?

Another argument I hear, exemplified by the politician mentioned above, is the following: His "actions when he was an underage teen are as he described them himself, 'inexcusable,' but that doesn't mean 'unforgivable.'" This argument negates the very real ramifications of a criminal act. A teenager can commit a crime. A teenager who kills someone is often tried in adult court. Besides, there is a vast difference between personal sexual experimentation and abusing five young girls. This is a serial offense, and it is deeply serious.

Our great God, with his upside-down kingdom economy, cares nothing about stature or fame or renown when it comes to violators like this. He will eventually enact justice, even if that means on the other side of eternity. The powerful who abuse others will not be able to maintain their image under the holy gaze of God.

This does not mean that those who perpetrate sexual crimes cannot confess their sins, truly repent, and find forgiveness. I would be serving a very small God if that were true. God's grace extends to victim and perpetrator alike. I cannot judge or know whether the son of the TV family has walked through deep, open repentance, nor is it my place to do so.

Still, sexual abusers' repentance does not permit the body of Christ to treat sexual crimes as nonissues, as personal family issues, or as something to be hush-hushed or locked behind a door of elders or church boards. When a church hears of sexual abuse, they must report the crime to the authorities, then let the chips fall where they may. Authenticity and sharing the truth in the light is the godly, proper way to deal with these kinds of situations. God's reputation is not marred when we dare to dignify the survivor, secure the help they need, send the perpetrator to get help (and punish him or her for a crime), and say, "Yes, this happened, and it was wrong."

It is a beautiful thing when churches grieve alongside survivors. It is a beautiful thing when the church lands on the side of justice. The psalmist wrote, "A judge who says to the wicked, 'You are innocent,' will be cursed by many people and denounced by the nations. But it will go well for those who convict the guilty" (Proverbs 24:24-25). May it be that we as followers of Jesus Christ, whose shoulders bore the weight of every sexual violation (oh, how it must have agonized him!), recognize and bring to light the evil that is sexual crime. May we go out of our way to be agents of healing for those who have been silenced for years, who shake and tremble to tell their stories, who feel they are crazy, or that their healing is taking too long, who struggle against feeling worthless and discarded. May we listen, dignify, and empathize. May we value the reputation of Jesus, who was both grace *and* truth. And in light of that, may we be agents of light, welcoming the truth.

NEW PRECEDENT

Earlier in 1992, a Colorado jury awarded over one million dollars to an Episcopal priest's rape victim. The survivor's attorney, Joyce Seelen, has handled 50 pastoral abuse cases in the past 20 years, with a gamut of denominations represented: Episcopal, Methodist, the Fundamental

Church of the Nazarene, and Church of Christ. "In my practice," she said, "I have not seen institutions taking steps to correct the problem. Every one of the churches that we've been successful against walked into court and said, 'We didn't know, and if we had known, we would have done something.' Over and over and over, what we saw was they didn't know because they didn't want to know."[13]

This is the centrality of the problem: We don't want to know. We don't want to believe these kinds of things happen in *our* churches. But they do. And we ignore the cries of the abused to our peril. A lethargic church that favors perpetrators to victims is an anemic one, but even more than that, it is an evil one. I write these words not as an angry survivor, but as one who has experienced the best the church has to offer. I healed because people in the church dared to listen to my story and pray for me. I write these words not to indict the church, but to rouse it to be better. I love the church.

An open letter to the leadership of the Roman Catholic Church by the staff of the *National Catholic Reporter* addresses this same desire to see a holy turnaround in our response to survivors. They write the following:

> This [argument] is not about debatable matters—celibacy or the filioque clause, or the primacy of Scripture or whether the Earth is the center of the universe or whether women should be allowed ordination or any of the hot button issues that have kept us roiling and at each others' throats these past decades. This, instead, is about a rot at the heart of the culture entrusted with leadership of the Catholic community. A rot so pervasive that it has touched every aspect of the community's life, disrupting all of the certainties and presumptions about who we are and who you are that helped hold this community together…You've been ensconced in a culture that has for too long protected you from the consequences of your worst instincts. The boundaries that once kept your culture safe from scrutiny have become as irrelevant today as the moats and walls of previous centuries. There is no hiding any longer. You've

been imbibing the excesses of power, authority and privilege that have accrued over centuries and, like the addict who hits bottom, a fundamental decision for recovery is essential to your survival.[14]

Rightly, this is seen as a failure of leadership over the millennia, a terrible rot, a scourge. Consider the thousands of survivors sacrificed on the altar of reputation protection. Consider how many crimes could have been prevented had the church taken sexual abuse seriously. The rot has not merely eroded the Catholic Church, but it has become pervasive in the Protestant church as well. When will we realize that God does not need us to preserve his reputation? He is not marred by our sin, but his reputation and the sullied reputation of the church is degraded by our silencing and cover-up.

INSTITUTIONAL PROTECTIONISM

Recently I watched the HBO Films movie *Paterno*. While it is not a documentary, the film torments the watcher with every single side of the sexual abuse "debate," especially when it comes to institutional protectionism. The entire movie grieved, triggered, and saddened me, especially knowing how long Sandusky's predation went on—decades—with so many victims in the wake, while people in power stood by, looking the other way. There, I observed the bravery of the survivor in 2008 who, worried far more for Sandusky's potential victims, essentially put his life on the line by testifying, by going first. This unshakable resolve cost him nearly everything. I admired Sarah Ganim, the reporter who doggedly pursued a story years earlier that no one seemed to care about. Despite dismissal and persecution, she continued uncovering the truth with tenacity and grit. I observed the sadness of Joe Paterno and his family as they faced the flagrant crimes of Sandusky.

In the haunting final scene, Ganim receives a phone call from a survivor. This is one of many, many calls she receives after the story breaks into the news cycle. She tells him, "There are a lot of people who have—have gone through this. I'm sure you know that...um, have you talked to anyone about this?"

"Well, the lawyer and…I talked to Joe."

"Joe…J-Joe Paterno?"

"We…we didn't really talk about it. He said that Jerry's a good man. That was pretty much it."

"Okay. And, um, do you, uh—do you remember when exactly it was that this—that this all took place?"

"Yeah. It was in summer. In 1976."

"Uh, I'm sorry. You said…1976?"[15] The movie ends starkly here.

Decades followed this disclosure of abuse.[16] How many victims were preyed on and assaulted after that disclosure? How many devastated lives would have been prevented had Paterno reported the abuse back then?

As you know, in the fall of 1972, I resembled this survivor. Though it is entirely not typical to report abuse when you're in the midst of it at five years old, *I told*. I cupped my babysitter Eva's ear and whispered the devastation to her. She knew, *but she did nothing*. Had she done something, *anything*, I would not have been devastated by months, *months*, of sexual attack by teenage neighbors and their friends. Had she told, perhaps I would have received trauma therapy. But even more importantly than that, the abuse would have stopped, and those boys would have faced consequences for their actions. Eva protected her institution—the daycare in her home. She erred on the side of her livelihood—the money she received from several parents to "watch" their children. She knew what was happening, she allowed it to continue, and she even pushed me out the doorway after I disclosed the abuse to her.

I would love to say that the church is different. I would love to say that Christian institutions and charities are different—that they rightly expose those who do harm. But so many times, those who know about abuse default to protectionism rather than justice.

It is sometimes harder for me to forgive Eva than it was for me to forgive those boys. She did not protect me, an innocent. By ignoring my plea for help, she not only devastated me, but also kept the door wide open for those boys to continue to perpetrate sexual violence, most likely for years. It cemented the narrative that I was unworthy of protection. How many more Marys were there because she failed to tell the truth? I get sick just thinking of it.

It is one thing to be duped by a predator; it is quite another to know about predation and do nothing. That is criminal because it allows for a criminal to continue to perpetrate. In my case and in many others, we see the insidious nature of institutional protectionism, where survivors are summarily dismissed while people in power are shifted around musical-chairs fashion, or never held to account at all, while an institution protects reputation (and, related to it, money) at the expense of the survivors.

Some would call talking about sexual abuse discoveries gossip. Others might call our efforts to expose predators a witch hunt. Still others force forgiveness as if it were a formula, to be performed robotically the very instant we hear of a predator's exposure. Others feel a perpetrator's job loss and loss of reputation is enough punishment. But what if we successfully prosecute Sandusky or Weinstein? Is that enough? The survivors will live with the memory of their violation their entire lives. They have ached in the silent hell of it for years. Some, like Sandusky's victim who first went on record, have to push to be heard, be exposed to ridicule and shame over and over again, and fight to be believed. Sometimes they even sacrifice their mental health for the sake of exposing the crime. This holy act of exposing crimes against innocent victims is the epitome of taking sin seriously. It's the raucous beauty of the cross, where Jesus sacrificed himself in order to set humanity free. So many survivors have done this, but our thanks to them often has been to push back or silence them.

Those who have been victimized are allowed to tell their stories. They are allowed their grief. They are allowed to process. They are allowed (and should be widely encouraged) to educate us on the perilous, conniving ways they were lured and harmed. We need their voices. We need their wisdom. We need their words. For them, talking about their experience does not indicate some sort of vendetta, vindictiveness, or spite; it is simply the release of years of shame into healthy air.

We should be mad. We should be allowed to be furious that predators get away with their crimes *for years*. We should seethe with righteous anger that people with respectable titles and positions heard of abuse and did nothing about it. It should keep us up at night.

Some would say naming names is wrong. But as I was reminded today in a thread on Facebook, Jesus (and Peter, Paul, and James) called people out by name, particularly false teachers—all for the sake of the purity of the people of God. (See 2 Corinthians 5:1-13; Galatians 2:11, 6:1; 2 Thessalonians 3:14-15; 1 Timothy 1:3-7: 5:20; Titus 3:10-11; James 5:19-20.)

To all those who told people in positions of power to stop the abuse and were dismissed: *I hear you, I see you, and I am so sorry.* That is not how it should have been, but it is what happened. That was wrong. The church, the ministry, the missions organization should have listened. They should have protected you. They should have gone to the authorities, who are better equipped to handle these cases, not kept it quiet and dealt with it in-house. They should have preferred you, one who is made in the image of God, over institutional reputation.

To those who try to silence a survivor because it is more convenient or too painful to hear the truth: Spend some time listening to a sexual abuse survivor. Hear their story and love them. If that person is a minor, report the abuse to the authorities. Don't be an Eva. If you keep it silent or summarily try to silence survivors, you become a painful part of their abuse story. Your silence makes you culpable. To not act is to act.

To the Christian institutions who are trying to balance their legal obligations, moral duty, and their desire for self-protection: Do the right thing. Repentance and apology can happen at a corporate level. And it must also happen person to person. Rapists should lose, not win. They should be caught, not coddled. They should be imprisoned, not passed along to different locales to rape again. Shuffling perpetrators around smacks the face of justice, mars the survivor's pathway to peace, and proves that the powerful, when they become intoxicated by their power, can enact the most evil violence upon others.

The frustration, though, comes when doing the math. Take one predatory person, perhaps hundreds of survivors, and 30 or so people working to uncover the truth, and you see how much time and how many resources it takes to uncover a crime. Those 30 for one predator. Now multiply everything by the protected predators who successfully sought asylum in their church structures. The cover-up is massive (and evil), but it will take a lifetime of reporters and good citizens to scratch the surface of the abuse. In this, I lament. The problem is just so large, and for so long, predators got away with their crimes.

No more. Please, no more. When bullies win, the entirety of society suffers—often silently. It is time to change the culture, to be open about what happened, dragging the perpetrator into the light and exposing the darkness. Let's call rape what it is: a murder that leaves its victim alive.[17]

Our churches must believe survivors over the clever pleas of so-called repentant rapists. We must strive to become a safe place for survivors and an unsafe place for predators. We must bravely report suspicious behavior. We must stop marginalizing survivors while providing havens for rapists. When we remove protection from rapists, the criminal justice system and the free press have the ability to perform their rightful civic duties.

As a church, we must welcome stories. When survivors dare to go first and tell their stories, they empower others to tell their stories, which then opens more doors for healing and justice. We must never underestimate the power of a story, even if the perpetrator goes free (mine did), because together we can help our church culture go from being silent—which empowers rapists—to being vocal. We must no longer tolerate institutions that blindly protect rapists. Let's work toward removing that protection by encouraging open and honest dialogue, dignifying survivors by listening to their stories, and praising the criminal justice system when it enacts justice. In short, let's be a part of a church that prosecutes rapists instead of protecting them. Let's not be guilty of Ezekiel's cautionary tale (34:1-11) written to the shepherds of Israel. Let these words sink in:

> Then this message came to me from the LORD: "Son of man, prophesy against the shepherds, the leaders of Israel. Give them this message from the Sovereign LORD: What sorrow awaits you shepherds who feed yourselves instead of your flocks. Shouldn't shepherds feed their sheep? You

drink the milk, wear the wool, and butcher the best animals, but you let your flocks starve. You have not taken care of the weak. You have not tended the sick or bound up the injured. You have not gone looking for those who have wandered away and are lost. Instead, you have ruled them with harshness and cruelty. So my sheep have been scattered without a shepherd, and they are easy prey for any wild animal. They have wandered through all the mountains and all the hills, across the face of the earth, yet no one has gone to search for them. Therefore, you shepherds, hear the word of the LORD: As surely as I live, says the Sovereign LORD, you abandoned my flock and left them to be attacked by every wild animal. And though you were my shepherds, you didn't search for my sheep when they were lost. You took care of yourselves and left the sheep to starve. Therefore, you shepherds, hear the word of the LORD. This is what the Sovereign LORD says: I now consider these shepherds my enemies, and I will hold them responsible for what has happened to my flock. I will take away their right to feed the flock, and I will stop them from feeding themselves. I will rescue my flock from their mouths; the sheep will no longer be their prey. For this is what the Sovereign LORD says: I myself will search and find my sheep."

The flock of God needs shepherds who will inconvenience themselves for the sake of the outcast, the broken, and the victimized. We need leaders who will feed us, not profit from our silence. We need a church that is proactive rather than reactive. We need leaders imbued with kindness, compassion, and empathy. We need actions to back up words. We need honesty about what has happened, not cover-up. We need leaders who will ask the question, "Why have so many left the church?" and then actively pursue them. We need shepherds who chase the wounded instead of chastising them. The last portion of Ezekiel above is haunting. If we fail to respond to the massive sexual abuse pandemic in our midst, God himself will tear down the structures that empowered abusive behavior. These leaders will be removed. God will clean his house.

PART THREE

SHAPING WHAT'S NEXT

CHAPTER NINE

A NECESSARY EDUCATION

If you preach the gospel in all aspects with the exception of the issues that deal specifically with your time, you are not preaching the gospel at all.

MARTIN LUTHER

There is still so much we do not know about the aftereffects of sexual abuse, but one thing is certain: This kind of soul-killing assault leads to trauma. And trauma has tentacles that reach into the survivor and persist. Once we understand the aftermath, we can better provide safe havens for those who suffer. This is not a one-and-done recovery: Simply pray this prayer, believe these verses, go to this conference, and all will be well. No, the healing journey stops and starts, and it takes a lifetime to walk. Walking with the wounded rarely fits into a program. As I mentioned in the introduction, it is the pure act of discipleship.

My own story includes this discipleship journey. From Young Life leaders in high school who listened to my story (with eyes wide!), to friends and church members in college who prayed and prayed and prayed (while I cried and cried and cried), to counselors I consulted in my thirties who helped me understand why it was hard for me to have sex, to prayer warriors I met in my forties whose Holy Spirit insight led to new levels of healing, to survivor advocates in my fifties whose work with others sparks a fiery zeal in me to do the same, I grew through my trauma toward health. I have the church and its beautiful members to thank. I know the positive influence Jesus's followers provided for my story—this is why I'm writing this book. During my long-term research about what people and churches face in becoming safe havens, I have unearthed seven crucial misunderstandings.

1. MISUNDERSTANDING TRAUMA'S EFFECT

First, let's take a deep dive into the impact sexual assault has on the human heart. These are adapted from my sexual abuse recovery book, *Not Marked: Finding Hope and Healing After Sexual Abuse.* The purpose of this list is twofold: to help with personal understanding and also with corporate empathy. In reading the following, those who have been victimized can find insight into their own stories and why they struggle today. Those who love survivors will gain a deeper understanding of those who suffer, providing much-needed empathy and help.

Some sexual abuse survivors:

- Are afraid, incapable, resentful, or wary of having sex, even in a committed, loving marriage.
- Struggle with feelings of inadequacy or guilt for not being "enough" for their spouse sexually.
- View sex as a commodity, not as a loving act.
- Are repulsed by the sexual act.
- Are, conversely, overly drawn to or addicted to sex or pornography.
- Are triggered easily, freeze, or disassociate during the sexual act.
- Truly believe the world is evil, and often succumb to hopelessness.
- Blame themselves constantly—particularly for being assaulted.
- Battle pervasive and debilitating shame.

- Have memory blocks for long periods of time.

- Practice self-contempt.

- Constantly long for their abuser to love them (in an appropriate manner).

- Gravitate toward abusive relationships because that is what is known and "safe."

- Struggle with suicide and suicidal thoughts.

- Cut themselves.

- Are thrown back to the event when their children reach the age they were when the abuse started.

- Overeat to prevent anyone from seeing them as sexual.

- Embrace entropy by believing that things will never get better; they'll only ever get worse.

- Deny what went on, refuse to talk about the past, and, instead, put on a mask to pretend all is well—often for decades.

- Detach from significant relationships, walking away when someone wants to break through.

- Feel held hostage by their bodies. Bodies often react even when the conscious mind is not actively thinking about trauma.

- Minimize the abuse, talking about other abuse as more "significant" than theirs. Some feel ashamed that they can't seem to get over something so insignificant.

- Worry that if they face the past, they'll die or fall completely apart.

- Feel used easily.

- Are addicted to approval.

- Have difficulties trusting others.

- Fear abandonment.

- Burst their anger—they keep it in so long and so well that, when emotions surface, they erupt.

- Worry that if they tell the truth, family members and/or friends will abandon them, especially when that truth disrupts a dysfunctional family or church system.

- Harbor deep resentment toward the person who chose not to protect.

- Must control everything.

- May have victimized others.

- Struggle with addiction—alcohol, opioids, food, drugs, anorexia/bulimia, screens, gaming, affairs, achievement, porn—all in secret.

- Believe they are marked for further sexual exploitation— that it's inevitable.

- Constantly fret that their children will be abused.

- Startle easily.

- Are desperately afraid of being alone.

- Experience flashbacks or nightmares or night terrors.

- Either take excessive risks or completely abandon risk.

- Are hypervigilant.

- Believe they are worthless.

- Overachieve to prove worth or rebel to gain attention.

- Coddle the belief that they are "different" from others— but not in a good way.

- Battle a pervasive feeling of not belonging.

- Are insecure.

- Never believe compliments.

- Are diagnosed with panic attacks, insomnia, dissociative disorder, conversion disorder,[1] bipolar disorder, or anxiety and depression.

- Are self-destructive and self-sabotaging.
- Face an autoimmune disease.
- Are petrified of doctors or counselors.
- Have a poor body image.
- Have been diagnosed with PTSD or C-PTSD (Complex Post Traumatic Stress Disorder).

Sexual trauma is difficult to overcome (though not impossible), no matter how severe it was. As mentioned above, survivors tend to minimize their abuse, comparing it to more extreme acts of predation. But healing takes a long time, whether the survivor has been "superficially" violated or harmed over a period of years. In some ways, we've all experienced violation. We are all on a healing journey—which is a truth that should empower any church wanting to come alongside. We're all in this together.

All told, sexual trauma gives rise to complex issues, which many face in our congregations today. Because we've become adept at minimizing our pain or neglecting to bring up our pasts (both distant and immediate), we sit alongside each other, oblivious to the burdens each bears—something some bear on a daily basis.

2. MISUNDERSTANDING WOMEN'S DAILY FEARS

In our violence-filled world, with a 24/7 news cycle that constantly focuses on brutal acts, it's no wonder people are terrified. But separate the sexes, and you'll find a chasm between the types of daily fears each faces. I used to chalk up my hypervigilance to my past, but I now understand that a majority of women leave the comfort of stores and go into darkened parking lots with trepidation. Some carry their keys firmly between each finger as a weapon and cross over to the other side of the road when they perceive threatening people coming their way. Others take self-defense classes. Some continually scope out safe places to escape to while walking down the street. Women check their car's backseat before getting in. Joggers carry mace or pepper spray and text their friends prior to a long run—just in case. Most won't answer the door if the doorbell rings. Some don't leave their homes at night, fearing what could happen. The list of precautionary measures is immense.

Novelist Margaret Atwood once asked a male friend in what ways men feel threatened by women. His reply? "They are afraid women will laugh at them." When she reversed the question, asking what about men threatened women, women responded, "We're afraid of being killed."[2] The evangelical church, saturated in male leadership, simply may not understand the fear half of their congregants suffer—daily.

3. MISUNDERSTANDING THE NATURE OF SIN

Sin is rebellion against God, but it is usually not an isolated act. Sin affects the tribe, and sometimes that sin is so damaging to people or the surrounding community that it is called a crime. Sin is birthed by evil, evil choices, and the devil himself. N.T. Wright has written extensively about the nature of evil: "Evil is the force of anti-creation, anti-life, the force which opposes and seeks to deface and destroy God's good world of space, time and matter, and above all God's image-bearing human creatures."[3] Anything that destroys a human being has sin as its root.

Part of sin is denial. Denying that sin has occurred, denying that it is significant, or brushing it off by saying *it happened so long ago* empowers perpetrators and demeans survivors. In one evangelical scandal I referred to earlier, where an older brother sexually assaulted his younger sisters and a babysitter, we see this denial in operation. The girls, according to the parents, were *barely* victims. The brother hardly touched them under their clothes, his father said—and that happened for only a few seconds. After all, other families had worse situations with "actual" rape, so they painted the crime as less serious. They talked to other families who said this kind of curiosity and sexual exploration was commonplace. Ironically, the brother touched his sisters more salaciously than any courting boy would be allowed (the family adheres to a strict view of courtship). Their dismissive statements ignore, diminish, and sideline the girls who did not choose to be touched.

After touching the girls, the boy confessed, according to his father, who said it had been very quick, and that the brother was grieved by his actions and told them immediately. Instead of camping on the sadness they felt over their daughters' violation, the parents shifted the focus to their son. "This isn't something we wanted to come out," the father said, "but if people can see that [our son], who did these very bad things when he was a young person, that God could forgive him for these terrible things, then I hope other people realize that God can forgive them and also make them a new creature."[4] The parents direct most of the empathy toward the one who violated. How tender his heart was to confess! How awful it was to casually involve the police. How bewildered those girls were who probably had no idea he even touched them. How unfair!

The mother quipped, "I know that every one of us have done things wrong. That's why Jesus came." The message becomes: *Nobody is perfect, so quit throwing those pesky stones, you who hate grace and demand justice. Instead, why not just throw the stones at our sinner selves?* When statements like this are applied to crimes, they take on a sinister bent. As Elizabeth Esther wrote, "When everything is evil, *nothing* is actually evil."[5] During this scandal, I read some disturbing comments suggesting that all men have rape fantasies, so, therefore, we should just offer this boy a little grace since we're all so awful. This kind of reasoning says, "We're all like this offender." However, a vast chasm exists between thinking about something horrific and actually carrying it out. Both are sin, but one is a punishable crime.

In the aftermath of the public revelations, the parents circled the wagons, playing the Christian-martyr card and then demonizing the "evil" media who covered the story. The mom said, "There is an agenda, and there are people that are purposing to try to bring things out and twisting them to hurt and slander."[6] She painted the situation not as a crime but as a spiritual battle, with gossip and slander being the weapons leveled against her family.

But this family entity was not the victim—their daughters were. This family experienced the expected fallout of their intentionally public life after a *crime* came to light. Jesus reminded us, "All that is secret will eventually be brought into the open, and everything that is concealed will be brought to light and made known to all" (Luke 8:17). This outing of blatant sin was actually a gift from the Creator, who loves truth and hates the crime of sexual assault.

We minimize sin when we fail to protect the most vulnerable from it. We pervert justice when we value the abuser over the abused. It is time we welcome those who uncover sexual crime in our midst—even in our families and, yes, our churches. It is time to stop dismissing what these sins of predation ushered in, vowing to stop uttering Christian clichés that minimize the supreme harm done.

Some Christian writers have even shifted blame from perpetrator to survivor, reversing the sin narrative. One even believed that children who were molested needed to confess their sin in order to be set free from the consequences of the other person's sin![7] Hear me: Being sinned against in such an evil manner (someone violating your will, heart, and body in a malevolent way) has nothing to do with your sin and has everything to do with the perpetrator's bent toward evil and victimization. Survivors must never be blamed for someone else's crime.

4. MISUNDERSTANDING FORGIVENESS

We like our formulas. We cast our well-loved clichés like apple seeds, thinking we're spreading the gospel to a dying world. After all, as I mentioned above, we all sin. And, therefore, we must all forgive—quickly, or we'll be in danger of bitterness. Sadly, how survivors respond to trauma has become a pet project of many in the church. There's an unwritten narrative that survivors must adhere to, and it goes something like this:

- Tell your story, but don't tell it too much, and be sure to highlight all the places God intervened.

- Admit your own sin—you shouldn't have worn that; that place you went to was an invitation to abuse; or you thought it was a date, so you trusted too early.

- Offer forgiveness to the predatory person quickly. After all, you wouldn't want to be guilty of your own sin by failing to forgive.

- Stop talking about the past. It's in the past. If you do share it, share it as a victorious testimony only, diminishing the effect of the violation.

The actual narrative looks nothing like this. It's not so simple to get over sexual violation. Recovery takes years of work, and forgiveness is not a one-time, easy decision, particularly if it is demanded or expected right away for the sake of peace and putting something shameful behind you.

Often, we see in communities of faith that survivors are admonished to be gracious, offering instant forgiveness to their abuser, as if it could be happily doled out like a trinket or cheap candy. And when someone is pressured to "be like Jesus" and forgive swiftly, this pressure often causes harm.

Sexual violation cuts deeply. As mentioned at the beginning of this chapter, it eats away at a person's sense of worth, esteem, and personhood, paving the road for future self-destructive behavior, suicidal thoughts, feelings of utter worthlessness, sexual dysfunction, guilt, shame, and all manner of disorders. The process of moving beyond the trauma of sexual violation is excruciating, long, and sometimes debilitating. The demand for instant forgiveness and the exhortation to "put it behind you" delays the healing process—a journey that begins only by stating the awfulness of the violation. By sweeping the story under the rug for the sake of one's family or church community, we may save the perpetrator's reputation and the reputation of those near him or her, but we lose important ground in becoming free.

Easy forgiveness may gloss over the terrible situation in the short term, but it reinforces for everyone the idea that the soul-siphoning sin committed against the victim was trivial and should be easy to get over. It forgets Jesus's strong admonition about millstones and people who hurt the vulnerable. I'm not advocating bitterness. And I fully welcome grace. God has the most beautiful ability to make beauty from ashes, and we are most like him when we extend forgiveness. But that healing must be allowed to take its course in due time and not be rushed, forced, or prescribed.

I first forgave the teenage boys who molested me as a five-year-old when I was in college, a decade and a half after they spent a year violating and demeaning me. In that moment, I believed, naively, that I was done, that I would never have to revisit the pain of that year. Instead, I found that healing happens in layers.

When I got married, my past trauma roared to life, and, once again, I had to choose forgiveness. I had to seek more counseling. My husband had to choose to forgive those boys too. Even today, when I suffer a flashback of memory, triggered by the constant stream of #MeToo news, I have to breathe out forgiveness. Forty-one years after my own trauma began, I finally had the courage to write a letter to the boys who molested me. But even so, I still get angry.

Those who know me see great redemption (thanks to Jesus, who took on my sin, the perpetrators' sin, and all sexual sin upon his shoulders). They see joy. They see a changed life. But I would be perpetuating a myth if I told folks it was simple and easy to get past my trauma—a sort of snap-your-fingers-to-forgiveness formula.[8] Every sexual abuse recovery narrative is different. It's shaped like the person who shoulders the story. Our best gift is to offer them space to forgive in their own sweet time, all through the gentle but compelling power of the Holy Spirit.

5. MISUNDERSTANDING OF RESPONSES TO ABUSE

The church as a whole has a naive understanding of the dynamics of sexual abuse disclosure. We are guilty of forcing ourselves, like Cinderella's brash sisters, into the ill-fitting shoes of survivors, declaring (callously) that we would do things differently. We wouldn't blame ourselves for the assault—unless, of course, we were "asking for it." Surely, we would have fled the scene. Given the same circumstances, we would have screamed for help or fought back. And certainly, we would have called the authorities immediately, welcomed a rape kit exam, and gone on our merry way. We would *never* wait decades to tell. In fact, those who wait so long are just looking for new pity for an old wound—meaning if you did not disclose soon after, you don't deserve to grieve today. Get over it, already! Isn't that the narrative of the gospel, that the old is gone? If you wallow in your pain, you must not believe in the power of the gospel like I do—I who would handle a sexual assault perfectly.

I'm sure you see my sarcasm in the paragraph above. But this is the response to many abuse survivors—particularly in the church. They're victimized by a sexual abuser, live in fear of people finding out, and then, when they finally share, they're revictimized by the insensitivity of others.

Why don't survivors respond in a so-called "perfect" way? For many logical, self-protective reasons, one of which involves stereotypes. Rape, historically, has been understood as a scary man stalking a woman walking down a dark street, or leering through her window at home, and then breaking in. But there are many forms of rape, and not all perpetrators are men. So if the survivor's narrative strays from the stalker-coming-through-the-window story, it may prevent him or her from sharing. *Maybe it wasn't rape,* they rationalize.

Because many victims freeze or dissociate during the act of predation, they question whether they assented to the assault. What might have been a natural, self-protective response (the body involuntarily shutting down or the mind mentally leaving a situation) can become the very reason a victim won't fight back in the moment.

The fear of not being believed is strong, and it has kept many, many people from telling their stories—something people criticize without understanding the psychology involved. One survivor of (now-convicted) Larry Nassar told her parents what he had done to her in the basement of his home, but Nassar convinced the parents she lied to them. She was not a gymnast, but a six-year-old girl whom Larry would assault for six more years. At one point, the girl's father, so convinced his daughter had lied, looked at her and told her he would make her life a living hell if she didn't finally come clean and tell the truth—that she had made it all up. She sank. She believed her father would do what he threatened, so she said that she lied about Nassar's many instances of abuse.[9]

Fear of social norms prevents many from disclosing abuse. Calling someone a rapist has dire consequences, and often rape occurs within a relationship—sometimes even in marriage. Bringing the crime to the surface ruins everything—the perpetrator's life, along with their social circle and their family. Besides, survivors have been taught that no one likes a tattletale.

The stigma of rape is strong all over the world. Some don't want to even name it because they don't want to be seen (or to see themselves) as weak or morally corrupt. Some believe that they are now "damaged goods." As long as they don't disclose the perpetration, their reputation will be intact.

Some are not able to begin healing because they seldom find themselves in safe, protective relationships. They sense (wrongly or rightly) that their significant relationships cannot endure the disclosure. Or they fear telling will taint the tenuous relationships they currently have. Many survivors fail to tell their potential life partner for this very reason.

Shame, as mentioned in chapter 4, plays a significant role as well. What a survivor endured was so dehumanizing that bringing that violation to light only highlights their pervasive sense of shame. Disclosing, in their mind, shouts their worthlessness to a world that has never been safe in the first place.

Retaliation is a tangible fear for many survivors. Perhaps their abuser has power and money. With the nature of predatory people and the way they tend toward excessive narcissism, anything that challenges the perpetrator's grandiose opinion of him or herself is an invitation to a fight. Some perpetrators launch public character assassination campaigns against their victims, while others are litigious, threatening legal and economic ruin to any who would come forward.

Some survivors have convinced themselves that the assault they experienced was inconsequential in the first place. By bringing it to light, they worry they'll be drawing attention to something that really had no effect on them. They cannot see the link between their current depression and anxiety and the past abuse, and they feel they should be over it by now.

A sense of low self-worth is another reason survivors deny their abuse. Maybe the survivor has been so beaten down by life's circumstances that they feel they deserved ill treatment. Why rock the boat? This is just their lot in life. This belief morphs into learned helplessness. They fear that nothing will ever improve, that more abuse is apt to come. They tell themselves to put their heads down and endure it—expect nothing more.

Survivors who were inebriated or drugged by a perpetrator have a hard time reporting to authorities because they have no recollection of what happened other than the physical evidence in the aftermath of the assault. They question if they even can come forward since they were unconscious during the violation.

Lastly, those who have been sexually harassed often don't disclose the abuse for economic reasons. If their superior at work is making suggestive comments or grabbing them inappropriately, to tell is to invite dismissal. Some in economically precarious situations have learned to tolerate sexually abusive behavior because they simply have no other option. They need their jobs to survive.

6. MISUNDERSTANDING COMPASSION

Compassion is powerful. Perhaps we haven't misunderstood it as much as we've stopped practicing it altogether. We're reminded by Paul that even God woos us with compassionate zeal: "Don't you see how wonderfully kind, tolerant, and patient God is with you? Does this mean nothing to you? Can't you see that his kindness is intended to turn you from your sin?" (Romans 2:4). Too often, we see the church err on the side of self-righteousness rather than selfless-righteousness. We have forgotten how to love the broken, preferring the echo chamber or our own opinions to washing the feet of those who struggle.

Advocate Jimmy Hinton tweeted, "Almost daily I'm thanked by survivors for being kind. It makes me sad and angry that you all receive any response other than kindness. Too many Christians have a bad habit of supporting abusers and destroying their victims."[10]

On my Facebook page, someone wrote this "apology" about my traumatic past:

> Sorry to hear about your trauma. We adults have the responsibility to get professional help if we are having

emotional issues. We adults have a responsibility to *not* wait almost 40 years before going to authorities. Myself and other women who are my dear friends we would have gone to authorities ASAP because none of us would have wanted another woman to go through our ordeal. I can assure you I know of no church body who is not compassionate and coming alongside those who have experienced what you write you have been through. Change churches.

She continued:

No matter how uncomfortable we may be, we *must* notify appropriate authorities at once if we women have been through trauma. It's called being responsible.[11]

This commenter knows very little about the nature of trauma, or the impact of predatory behavior and the fear that victims experience in the moment of the actual assault. Contrary to her assumptions, I did tell—but nothing happened. I have pursued and chased healing most of my adult life. I am doing better than before. I'm not fully healed, but I am healing, and have experienced so much growth. My anger comes not from my own story but on behalf of those who are in the early stages of their healing, who are being threatened, berated, and eviscerated on social media simply for telling their stories. Unfortunately, many survivors face self-aggrandizing vitriol when they dare to begin the process of disclosure.

The church often speaks like this commenter. She failed to demonstrate true compassion—the marriage of both truth (which she embraced) and grace (which she did not). I was tempted to engage in a tit for tat with her, but as I prayed about it and let my heart rate return to normal, I prayed for her. "Thank you that you have changed her story. Thank you for giving her insight into the importance of moving on. Renew her mind tonight. Help her to walk in your shoes tonight, deeply empathizing with the broken as you did when you walked this earth. Bless her with joy as she goes to sleep. Bring her life and peace as she wakes up. Amen." After that prayer, she wrote nothing further.

7. MISUNDERSTANDING WHAT THE CHURCH IS

To our detriment, we believe the church to be a building full of self-possessed people who rarely struggle without an accompanying victory story. But the church is simply this: a people called out, who have allowed the redemption of Jesus to wash over them. We *all* have broken stories, but our wrecked state is not something to retreat from, but the impetus for finding Jesus. No one is better than anybody else. Leaders are simply people who serve and equip the body of believers to serve as well. The hierarchy is a mutual subjugation beneath Jesus, the head of our endeavors. We must have the mind of Christ, and when we do, we begin to act like him.

The church, the ones who have been called, the mercifully forgiven—we are to be the hands and feet of Jesus on this earth. We are not corrupted or enticed by political position. We are not enthralled with power or might, but take delight in embracing the weak. We understand that we serve Jesus when we love those who are hurting. We find Jesus in the face of the sexual abuse survivor. We hear his voice trumpeted by the frail. We taste God's goodness when we say grace over a meal with the humble. We sense him saying, "Well done, good and faithful servant," when we serve those whose stories are shattered. The church is not a place of perfection. It is, and should be, a haven of protection.

CHAPTER TEN

A NUANCED CULTURAL SHIFT: FROM HOW-TO TO #METOO

*Me too. I was 7 he was a sweeper in my school. I was 11 he was my friend's
father. I was 13 he was my tuition teacher. I was 14 he was an old man
in a DTC bus. I was 16 he was a biker at a red light. I was 18 he was a
man at the bar of a pub. I was 21 he was a man at the railway station. I
was 23 he was a man in the metro. I was 24 he was my "best friend."*

TAMANNA YADAV[1]

When I first told a family member about what happened to me at five (ten years later), I picked at a hangnail till it bled. Bile bit my throat. She was the first I told, the first to whom I let out the desperately sad story of what those teenage boys did to me. Initially, she pushed back. Refused to believe such a shocking tale. Told me I must've been mistaken. That I believed it wrong.

So desperate for someone—*anyone*—to believe me, 15-year-old me told the story again.

And again with precise, awful details.

And again with names named and locations disclosed.

Until my family member finally believed.

But my victory of belief was short-lived when her rhetoric changed from disbelief to chastising me for not coming forward sooner. I was to blame for my tardiness. If only I had told back then, she would have rescued me. How was she to know those boys weren't trustworthy? (I wanted to say, "This is not about you," but I held my tongue.) Her next, nearly immediate tack was to whiplash into an armchair psychologist, telling me to go to counseling to get fixed. In that moment, I felt unbelieved, unheard, blamed, and utterly damaged. It's no wonder it took a few more years to let the story out again.

One of the most demeaning experiences a sexual abuse survivor can have is to be lectured instead of loved. We are not problems to be fixed or inconveniences to endure. We are not naive. We have searched for help, often ending in frustration. We've experienced the kind of patronizing interaction Richard Rohr warns against: "We mustn't lead with our judgments and fears. We shouldn't lead with our need to fix and solve problems. This is the agenda-filled calculating mind that cannot see things through God's eyes."[2]

At a West Coast writing conference, I had a conversation with a fellow writer. Something she said resonated with me: "We used to write how-to books." She mentioned a shift from how-to to #MeToo. For so long, our Christian living titles populating Christian bookstore shelves were didactic: how to be a better Christian in seven easy steps, formulas for parenting, tactics to have a better marriage. How to this. How to that. Christianity had been conveniently dissected into little steps of obedience in a neat, chronological order. Follow the steps, then find freedom. Simple! Easy! And binding.

CORRECTIVE CULTURAL SHIFT

But a shift has happened in our midst in the past few years, and it wasn't merely birthed from the #MeToo hashtag. It's a cultural shift, a corrective against spiritual formulas and all-is-well facades. We've begun to realize that you can't grow spiritual fruit in a lab. Formulas are inadequate for the process of the messy growth we experience in real life. And formulas seldom save; instead, they enslave—because if you struggle, then you're the problem. You haven't followed the steps correctly. In the past, if you didn't "grow" right, you blamed yourself. You saw all the clichéd frameworks that you failed to execute and self-chastised. You simply couldn't follow the rules properly. (This smacks of man-made religion and borders on excessive legalism.) Or perhaps you followed the seven easy steps, only you *still* feel suicidal or trapped or confused. Even when you did everything perfectly, you failed—which then led you to question the goodness of God—a logical thing to do. Because why wouldn't he answer your prayers? You did everything right!

But growing in relationship with God is never a formula. And sexual assault refuses to heal in a formulaic way. It often feels like an unsolvable equation.

Our lives are wildly creative and nuanced and different. We all have stories laced with pain and joy, hope and despair, failures and victories. Since we are so varied, wouldn't it follow that our ways of growing would be varied too? And when we compare our healing journeys to the pathway of others, we end up with questions like...

- "Why do I keep doing this one thing—the very thing I hate?"

- "Why does everyone else seem to fall into line, get with the program, and live perfectly acceptable lives while I struggle so much?"

- "Why am I the only one who questions or worries or balks at sappy Christian platitudes?"

- "Why doesn't anyone else seem to struggle with life?"

- "Why can't I just get over my sexual assault and be done with it? Lord knows, I've tried."

We used to write how-to books because that's what we thought would help others, but now authors are writing #MeToo books—and not just about sexual abuse, but about everything. We're telling our stories; we're reading stories. Memoir and personal experience have become more enticing than books of spiritual formulas. We do this because we're weary of formulaic, one-size-fits-all religion, and the longing for the wild story of God's great, continuing redemption can no longer be tamped down. We need to know we're not alone. We need to find community in our stories. Lists cannot ultimately change a heart, but stories can. My life has been radically altered by stories. Through stories, I found out I wasn't the only person to be violated sexually. Through stories, I know I am not alone in my struggle with body image or triggering when I least expect it, or startling easily. I know that many people in the big, wide world share similar insecurities, hopes, and wishes.

God has his own "Me too" moment. The Lord gave us statutes and laws, but humanity—enslaved to sin—could not keep them. The law simply pointed to our inability to save ourselves. It created longing for a better story, a redemptive one. Enter Jesus—not spectacularly, but in the nonenviable body of a dependent infant. Almighty God slipped into the skin of a baby. That baby grew up to live life alongside us, walk dusty pathways, grieve loss, experience betrayal, watch sunsets, harbor disappointments, and be abused. He tabernacled among us, pitching his tent on our soil, so that whatever trials or temptations or despairs we face, he can always say, "Me too." His example is our example. Words manifested as the Word-became-sinew—which is a beautiful analogy for the sexually abused. We share our devastating words, but we need actions to follow. Jesus spoke life-altering words, but he backed them up with redemptive action—not only on the cross (though I'll live my entire life in gratitude for that) but through the way he loved people. He epitomized the power of words married to loving action.

Telling our stories to safe people is a powerful practice. We go first so others can say #MeToo. We tell those stories not to water down the gospel but to elevate it to its proper magnificence—that God loved us so much that he made himself flesh, becoming empathetic and available to us. I still struggle against laws and statutes. I still make lists trying to be a better me. But I grow best in relationship, both with my Creator, who loves me enough to live in this world, and alongside all who bear his image. We are all just pilgrims on a rocky path, doing our best, failing, getting back up again, embracing grace, praying for the broken, and along the way telling the great, great story of our redemption.

HOW WE CHANGE OUR MINDS

Facts seldom change anyone's mind, but stories do. James Clear, author of the book *Atomic Habits*, wrote a fascinating article entitled "Why Facts Don't Change Our Minds." His premise is that we typically don't make a radical change in our thinking unless someone who is similar to us persuades us through relationship. He writes, "Facts don't change our minds, friendship does."[3] We are seldom influenced by people on the very opposite of the opinion spectrum, but we will consider information from someone close to us who also happens to share many of our beliefs. If this hypothesis is true, then the church can and should be a perfect place for us to reconsider some of our assumptions.

To change people's minds about how we can respond to the sexual abuse crisis redemptively, we must return to storytelling, friendship, and building relational capital. Clear elaborates:

> Convincing someone to change their mind is really the process of convincing them to change their tribe. If they abandon their beliefs, they run the risk of losing social ties. You can't expect someone to change their mind if you take away their community too. You have to give them somewhere to go. Nobody wants their worldview torn apart if loneliness is the outcome. The way to change people's minds is to become friends with them, to integrate them into your tribe, to bring them into your circle. Now, they can change their beliefs without the risk of being abandoned socially.[4]

In short, we must be the church to each other—to listen, befriend, invite. Social change doesn't happen after facts are put forward; it happens in the warm context of community.

We experienced the power of the table when we lived in France as church planters. Every week, sometimes several times a week, we invited people over to share a meal with us. We would spend our dinners discussing both light and difficult topics. Sometimes we would argue because the French tend to love debate. Some of our French friends even would change their opinion to the opposite one just to see if they could articulate the other belief. As an American, I found the whole situation untenable. If a friend argued, then it meant they didn't like me, and we would no longer be friends. If someone "won" an argument, then someone else "lost" it. It was then that I realized how competitive our culture was—in our society there must be a clear delineation between winner and loser—never a joyful sigh that we had an excellent argument. One winner. One loser. One who felt self-satisfied. One who walked away, head down. But our French friends would leave our table satisfied after a good discussion, and then kiss-kiss our cheeks and be on their merry French way, friendship intact. They understood that good relationships mean lively debate, and that a different opinion didn't mean we had to break off the relationship.

Sadly, in our social-media crazed culture, we have forgotten that human beings exist behind the pixels. Our ability to argue intelligently among friends has been lost. We don't sit around dinner tables much anymore, and because of that, we're polarized, isolated in our own camps about hot issues—even how to respond to sexual abuse, which should be a simple topic. "Sexual abuse is wrong. We should do something about it"—surely we can agree on that much. But because of heated rhetoric and segregated camps, we tend to demonize those with different opinions rather than listen and learn. If we would just break bread together as the early church did in Acts chapter 2, I wonder if we'd begin to see that people of differing opinions are not enemies, but fellow partakers. It's hard to hate someone with whom you share a meal. We must become more like Abraham Lincoln, who is purported to have said, "I don't like that man. I must get to know him better."

THE PROBLEM OF CONFIRMATION BIAS TODAY

One of the most difficult trials to endure is being unfairly judged and misunderstood. And no matter what you do to try to convince someone otherwise, your efforts only seem to prove your "guilt." I experienced this on Twitter one day where a man assumed that because I was pro sexual abuse survivor, I automatically had a slippery view of Scripture. He publicly accused me of dismissing the Bible. His belief fueled this exchange, utterly convinced he was right and that I was a heretic. Though the interchange became a blip in my life (I invited him and his wife for dinner because I felt these kinds of discussions were better had over a good meal), I understood just how powerful someone's initial assumptions about a person can become. They're nearly fixed, particularly in today's world where we judge first, then backpedal later.

In light of this shift away from actual connection toward superficial assumptions, it's important to talk briefly about the power of confirmation bias, and how it has harmed sexual abuse survivors over the millennia. When we suffer from confirmation bias, we interpret everything through our existing lens of how we think life works. What that means is this: When confronted with evidence to the contrary of hard-and-fast beliefs, it's nearly impossible to change them. Instead, we reframe what we hear to fit our known narrative. That's why it's very hard to reconcile sexual abuse, particularly by well-loved clergy. The belief is this: Pastors are to be trusted; they represent God. And even if they "fail," they deserve to be trusted again.

Confirmation bias is also why some people will not be persuaded by valid facts because to do so would mean alienation from their tribe (which believe otherwise, despite hard evidence) and a complete dismantling of personal beliefs. But before we vilify those who succumb to confirmation bias, it's vital to note that the condition has a positive root: hope. We want to live in a happy world that we understand. We want to believe that the world makes sense, and that our personal discernment of a friend can be trusted. If our confidant is caught in what he or she calls an indiscretion, we jump to believe their narrative. We have trusted and walked alongside this person, and we believe our view of him or her is correct. To consider the alternative means we have to face a chaotic world where people who appear to be upstanding are hiding heinous sins. To let go of the all-is-happy narrative means plunging into deep fear.

Confirmation bias and the need to believe in the goodness of all people is why Larry Nassar duped hundreds of parents, hiding his predation even while they were in the same room. He was known as the "nice guy." He treated some patients for free. So many people had touted his credentials. When the *Indianapolis Star* investigation first came to light, many people were shocked, then staunchly defended Nassar. Surely this upstanding citizen wouldn't harm women and girls! But he had hundreds of victims who soon found their voices. Confirmation bias simply could not withstand the onslaught.

While some malign the #MeToo movement with snide comments and a tantamount fear of the rise of false accusations, many of those victimized have now found their voices. One story ushers in hundreds of new stories. One brave account becomes many, and, as a result, those who felt utterly alone now feel camaraderie against a heinous evil. While reading tips and tricks of getting over trauma may have brought a smidgen of insight, hearing another *story* has sparked a movement of men and women who now actually believe a healed heart is possible.

When we find each other, we grow. We commiserate. We compare notes. We categorize sexual abuse correctly—as evil and wrong. We call churches, ministries, missions organizations, places of employment, and educational structures to account. We confound darkness by reveling in the light. Together, we heal. Together holds power. Together is safe community that salves the wounds of the broken.

CHAPTER ELEVEN

A NEW PATHWAY FORWARD

Trauma is the mission field of our time.

DR. DIANE LANGBERG[1]

O ur mission field beckons, and as Dr. Langberg eloquently states above, that mission field is trauma survivors. The field before us is ripe for harvest (because of the sheer enormity of those traumatized by sexual assault), but the empathetic, trauma-informed shepherds are few. Let's pray together that God would send these workers, and as we make such a daring ask, let's leave room for the possibility that we could be the answer to that fervent prayer.

I asked people all over the world what needed to be done about the sexual abuse crisis as it pertained to the church, and they answered. Their reflections form the framework for this chapter.

While it may seem overwhelming to tackle this issue, it's simply a reflection of good theology. In a letter dated November 8, 2018, the Bishop of London wrote the following to all licensed clergy in the Anglican Church: "Safeguarding from abuse, and responding well to abuse when it happens, are grounded in the fundamental themes of Christian theology and should be woven into the fabric of the culture of the Church. Churches are called to be places where all are welcome into open and secure communities that make known Christ's reconciling peace."[2] Even if we are not all Anglicans, this is a fitting mandate, a righteous calling, and a just response to a God who bears the scars of the broken. It reveals the shepherding mandate for leadership, to rightly care for and protect the sheep in its care.

ERR ON THE SIDE OF BELIEF

Detective Andrea Munford, one of the key people who brought Larry Nassar to justice, has an important philosophy of investigation: "Start by believing."[3] Telling a secret like this is belittling, scary, and traumatic. In the vast majority of cases, when a survivor tells their story, it can be believed. False reports are rare. In order to ensure someone isn't retraumatized by our responses, we should listen without judgment, asking clarifying questions when necessary, and offering extreme empathy. Survivors are not criminals; let's stop treating them like they're the ones being interrogated. Sarah[4] wrote this: "Ask for our story in whole before assuming the accused is innocent. Please stop assuming we are lying. Please stop bullying us because we are accusing one of your 'friends.'"

DON'T BYSTAND

Bystanders who choose to look the other way and not get involved cause irreparable harm to survivors. This is the exact opposite of what a good shepherd would do. A good shepherd would stop to save an exposed or endangered lamb. He or she would not ignore their bleats. Our collective silence has killed the resolve of many, leaving them vulnerable to further predation. Often the sexually abused have a more difficult time forgiving those who knowingly stood by but did nothing—and this certainly goes for church leadership that covers up, minimizes, or does nothing, or, in the worst cases, continues to empower the predator. Yes, there is a real fear of getting involved, of upsetting the order of things. We fear the consequences of intervening. We ask, "What if I am wrong?"

But what if we're right?

As followers of Jesus Christ, the defender of the broken and vulnerable, we are all mandatory reporters. We can no longer think that someone else will report abuse—it is up to us. We may know that what we see is wrong, but we backpedal in fear. Maybe we misunderstood? No, we must err on the side of protecting a victim, knowing that stopping one predatory person could also prevent dozens of other victimizations. With the commonly held statistics of one in four women and one in six men being sexually abused, that's a vast number of people who could have used a defender, a hero—a gutsy bystander who inconvenienced him or herself for the sake of the victim.

LISTEN TO SURVIVORS

One of the best (and easiest) interventions we can provide involves no speaking, no action, no mental wrangling. We simply listen. That's it. As active listeners, as the conversation continues and the survivor is comfortable, we may ask for clarification, but mostly we let our ears do the talking. Inserting ourselves and our biases into a disclosure conversation only muddies it. Chautona cautions, "Sometimes, the assumption of sin silences a victim. When a young woman shows up pregnant, it doesn't necessarily mean she was promiscuous, and when you assume sin without counsel and dialogue, some young women will keep their mouths shut."

James 1:19 rightly counsels, "Understand this, my dear brothers and sisters: You must all be quick to listen, slow to speak, and slow to get angry." But too often we reverse the order, becoming slow to listen, quick to speak—and when we speak, we inflict harm with clichés and ill-informed platitudes. Consider some of these insensitive retorts survivors have heard:

- "That was so long ago. You should be over it by now."
- "Because you still struggle with this, it proves you haven't given it to God. You are in disobedience by not letting go of the past."
- "God won't put you through more than you can bear."
- "Just choose joy. If you don't, you're not walking well with God."

- "It's your fault that you were harmed because…of what you wore, that it was on a date, or where you stood at the moment."
- "If you don't heal in the manner I prescribe (or that worked for me), then you are obviously in sin."
- "Just give it to God."

Jen shared one of the statements that had been flung her way: "'I'm just so shocked that happened to you because you seemed so strong.' In other words, only weak people get abused. It's subtle survivor shaming." Catz Meow tweeted, "The best was when the church showed up in numbers when my son's molester was arraigned, and defended him." Can you hear the anguish? Sense the frustration? Kelly tweeted her experience: "'What did you do to deserve that?' when I told a female church leader about the abuse I experienced by my mother—starting when I was 11 months old."

If we would simply listen and not speak, we would usher in a wave of empathetic healing in our churches.

DON'T TAKE THE EASY EXCUSE PATH

Some decide to either investigate or negate a sexual abuse claim because of the "easy" excuse that false reporting is a major issue. On the contrary, false sexual abuse claims make up about 6 percent of sexual abuse disclosures.[5] Don't let your fear of a false story prevent you from protecting those who have been preyed upon. Intervention and listening must trump inaction.

AVOID PRESCRIBING A HEALING JOURNEY

Each of us is unique. Therefore, our healing journeys are unique. To cram someone into your model of the appropriate way to "get over" sexual abuse is a judgmental and unfair act. In Lisa Grace's case, someone must have believed going to the police would harm her healing journey. She cautions:

Don't just pray for me. Don't just say, "Wait on God about going to the police." Please say you see me, that you see this is a crime. Encourage me to go to the police, not dismiss the idea, as maybe you should forgive and move on. Don't tell me that if I leave your church, no one will be there for me. Because I'm so broken. Tell me, please, that I'm broken because a crime was committed against me, and my body is evidence of the crime scene.

We must allow survivors their pathway without insisting on our own biased timeline of reporting and healing. Our job is to support, indicating we will be there throughout the ordeal, no matter how the survivor chooses to proceed. We have to remember that someone traumatized is not thinking linearly—they need support, not advice; empathy, not prescribed pathways; listening, not a soliloquy of shoulds.

Sylvia writes about her own interactions, particularly about the timeframe of healing: Don't treat the survivor as though she or he is dirty. If you believe that Jesus makes all things new, then believe that about the survivor too. But don't use that truth to shut the survivor's mouth. There is a point at which the survivor needs to stop rehearsing victimhood, but only God and the survivor can determine that point. Survivors sometimes inappropriately disclose, especially if they come from very dysfunctional families, so be gentle…Don't set deadlines on healing.

The most powerful response is not to prescribe anything, but simply commiserate. Bethy writes, "Be thoughtful of words and adages that sound good but lack a true understanding of the depth of concern. The best response I got from a preacher friend after my diagnosis was, 'Well, damn.' Yep. About sums it up." To commiserate is to shepherd well.

DON'T MINIMIZE THE ABUSE

I remember hearing about a friend walking through deep grief after losing several loved ones in a year, only to be patronized by another friend who said, "Yeah, I know how you feel. My cat died last year." Sexual abuse is traumatic. If you haven't walked through it yourself, don't assume you know how soul crushing it is.

We must also be careful in the language we use. Sexual abuse is not the same as a consensual affair. It is not the result of a casual indiscretion. Evie cautions:

> The presence of any power differential immediately means that consent is not fully possible…When consent is not fully possible, terms like relationship, indiscretion, and phrases like "She must have wanted it," or "It takes two to tango," or calling it "a slip-up," all of that nonsense needs to be thrown out the window.

EDUCATE YOURSELF AND YOUR CONGREGATION

With a little research, we can learn how to love those who battle the traumatic aftereffects of abuse. Heather Davediuk Gingrich, a counselor of 35 years, reminds us,

> Giving care to abuse survivors is not easy, particularly when church staff or lay helpers do not understand why survivors think, behave, or relate in certain ways. Simplistic solutions are sometimes offered in an attempt to bring about constructive change, but can frustrate helpers if their suggestions do not work and further damage survivors.[6]

She then advocates for clergy and lay education about abuse, the use of support groups, the importance of lay counseling, mentoring, coaching, and spiritual direction, and the need to provide helpful resources within and outside of the church community. Many churches now offer counseling on site, but it must be noted that not all counselors are adept at sexual abuse recovery or trauma-informed practices.

Elisabeth wants to see people become empowered about trauma. She writes: "Become trauma informed. Educate staff on the nature of traumatic memory. The science validating it is abundant. Understand that behavioral reactions to trauma are normal and designed into our brains by the Creator. These normal reactions may make the survivor appear unstable, but that instability is due to trauma and should be met with loving care, not suspicion." When we are educated about trauma, we will be less willing to judge how a survivor processes their abuse. We can become more empathetic with education.

Alyson emphasizes the power of being proactive. She writes, "Prepare ahead of time, practice godly loving responses, develop a team dedicated to handling disclosures, purposefully love survivors. Be willing to 'leave the ninety-nine' to save and protect the one who is vulnerable." She encourages churches to enact policies ahead of time, anticipating future disclosures. When the inevitable occurs, instead of reacting in crisis, the church can then simply follow the pathway they've already created.

Sexual education, while controversial in a Christian setting, must be part of our families' dynamics. Children need to know accurate names of body parts, what they can expect when they mature, what sex is, and what are appropriate boundaries. They need to know that no one should ever ask them to keep a secret (unless, perhaps, it's to surprise Daddy with a new fishing rod). Many young sexual abuse victims do not realize that what they are encountering is wrong or abusive because they have not been taught simple facts about reproductive organs. If we shy away from educating our children out of fear or the creep factor, we leave them vulnerable to predatory behavior. While we cannot completely protect our children, we can give them the very best chance at escaping a predator's grasp, and we can provide the kinds of homes that foster honesty and openness. While churches may not be involved in this particular aspect of education, they can certainly provide resources for families walking through these kinds of difficult and frank discussions.[7]

We teach children to trust people automatically, especially in a church setting. We tell children to give Uncle Charlie a hug, or blindly follow that youth group leader. We strip children of their autonomy when we insist that they be kind to elders (anyone who is older than they are is an elder). We forget that charm woos children. Boz Tchividjian warns, "The power of charm is a deadly weapon in the hands of someone who is targeting to abuse and misuse somebody else." He has taught his children, "Never obey blindly. Question authority."[8] When we add God to the mix, we fall into spiritual abuse. Saying things like, "God always wants you to obey your leaders," opens up anyone to the possibility of abuse. We forget about the power of the sanctuary platform to persuade people. That platform can blind us to character flaws, and just because someone has a position of authority does not prove they can be trusted.

EXPECT PUSHBACK

Sometimes the very people you would never expect to be perpetrators are, and when you expose them, there will be fireworks. When you speak truth to power—even within the church—you will be persecuted. Instead of reeling from the pushback, rejoice. This shows you really are walking with Jesus, the One who takes up the cause of the neglected. As Paul instructs Timothy, "Don't despair. Yes, and everyone who wants to live a godly life in Christ Jesus will suffer persecution" (2 Timothy 3:12). Your standing up reveals the Spirit within you: "If you are insulted because you bear the name of Christ, you will be blessed, for the glorious Spirit of God rests upon you" (1 Peter 4:14). By protecting the innocent and pulling down abuse structures that thrived in darkness, you are aligning yourself with the prophets: "Be happy about it! Be very glad! For a great reward awaits you in heaven. And remember, the ancient prophets were persecuted in the same way" (Matthew 5:12).

We cannot forget that pushing against sexual abuse and shedding light on perpetrators is spiritual warfare. Sexual abuse is war, and you are one of many warriors, fighting to end this awful injustice. And when you engage in this kind of warfare, the enemy of our souls will fight back—often through other Christians who will slander, malign, abuse, threaten, and seek to devour you. When I've encountered this kind of onslaught, I remind myself of this truth: "Stay alert! Watch out for your great enemy, the devil. He prowls around like a roaring lion, looking for someone to devour. Stand firm against him, and be strong in your faith. Remember that your family of believers all over the world is going through the same kind of suffering you are" (1 Peter 5:8-9). This is a global epidemic, a global suffering. You are not alone in your fight. And in the midst of that global fight, you are battling a defeated foe. James 4:7 encourages us to fight through submission—to God: "So humble yourselves before God. Resist the devil, and he will flee from you." Just as a cockroach scatters when the light is turned on, so does the devil have to flee when the name of Jesus (who is light personified) is spoken. Don't grow weary. Keep fighting.

PROTECT SURVIVORS, NOT REPUTATIONS

Jesus does not need his reputation protected. His glory is assured. His renown is settled. The church will grow when it brims with truth, not when it covers up misdeeds. And to the degree that a church lovingly shepherds and empowers survivors is the degree to which it will actually grow—not in numbers, which can be deceptive, but by depth of spiritual growth. Reputation management tends to be more about fear of losing money than protecting the church, and it's rooted in a theology of protectionism. Rachael Denhollander iterates,

> Churches believe they're doing the right thing, acting biblically, when in reality they're creating a toxic environment for the abused. If you bring attention to these errors, they believe they're being persecuted. They close their ranks tighter. It is tougher to get the Church to do the right thing than even secular institutions, because in churches they believe they're "just being obedient to God."[9]

But to be obedient to God means doing the godly work of loving others, protecting the vulnerable, and humbling ourselves.

BE HONEST

Pride and fear are what prevent honesty. Churches, ministries, and missions agencies want others to believe they are truly following the mandates of Christ. If they uncover something devastating—like sexual abuse in their midst—they tend to close their ranks tighter, as Denhollander aptly states above. Protection is nearly deified. After all, reputations are at stake, and if reputations are at stake, so is funding. But I would argue that this shortsighted, even satanic strategy will backfire. We're guilty of playing the short-term game without looking ahead to the long term. The Catholic Church is experiencing a massive loss of funding today—all because of cover-ups yesterday.

As stated earlier, some argue that being honest about abuse is gossip, but I would contend that it's not gossip to tell the truth for the sake of protecting the innocent. Honesty must be our hallmark. Why? Because it shows that an institution is far more interested in doing what is right and protecting the marginalized than they are about protecting their status. Jessica reminds us of the importance of disclosure—for the sake of the rest of the congregation: "When victims come forward, the leadership should tell the congregation so that any other victims can be found [in order to get] the help they need. Stop saying that it's out of respect for the victims that the congregation and parents aren't informed."

Honesty also means that leadership takes responsibility for any failures in the system. I would much rather read a heartfelt letter by a pastor admitting he or she missed something than a slick PR-firm "mistakes were made" missive. Jeanette encourages, "Publicly take responsibility for any red flags you overlooked or warnings you ignored. Whatever you do, do not follow 'I believe and support you' with a request for the victim to keep her story quiet. It is her story to tell, and she needs to tell it in order to fully heal."

One such honest disclosure involved a man who erotically rubbed the feet of congregants. The church responded, then communicated this to the congregation:

> At the April Stated Meeting of Presbytery at Westminster Presbyterian Church, Martinez, on Tuesday April 17, the Savannah River Presbytery voted to depose Brad Waller from Gospel ministry, for the abuse of power against minors and young men under his care, for the purpose

of auto-erotic stimulation derived from foot rubbing, to which he confessed before the court [presbytery].[10]

Pastor Robert Cunningham found out about the abuse that had happened in his congregation in the distant past. He wrote:

> Upon receiving this news from Savannah, we obviously became very concerned over the possibility that similar abuse took place while Brad was on staff at TCPC. We wrote an email to our congregation informing them of the situation and inviting them to an information meeting. After sending this email, we began receiving phone calls, emails, and social media messages from people sharing stories of abuse that took place while Brad was a pastor at TCPC.[11]

Ten days later, he made sure he conferred with the elders and pastors.

> We held a meeting of our session (board of elders), hired an attorney to walk us through the process, and hosted a congregational meeting to inform our people of the news and answer questions they may have had. We reported to and met with the police, and based on the latest information, they are currently not choosing to investigate. If more information surfaces, and the police choose to re-open the investigation, we will fully cooperate. In addition, our session has made a very significant institutional decision that we need to make you aware of: we unanimously voted to seek a third-party independent investigation.[12]

This is an example of a church whose leadership chose honesty over protection. They chose the survivors over a victorious story. They chose to do the right thing, no matter what the consequences might be. This kind of honest response promotes trust.

Allowing a perpetrator who is a leader in the church to slip away into retirement is also not honest. Evie cautions,

> The whole "He just needs to retire" is *not* effective, nor does it show any kind of repentance. If we're talking about a

pastor, then they need to publicly repent and/or the leadership needs to explain publicly why he has been removed. Not retired, not stepped down, but he has been removed— and why. The why needs to be clear it was not just an indiscretion. It was an abuse of power. Period.

GET ANGRY, BUT NOT AT THE SURVIVOR

When one woman came forward about a well-known megachurch pastor's sexual misconduct, she knew he would deny her allegations. But she did not expect that the leaders of the church would defend him during a family meeting in March of 2018. "After the family meeting, the evangelical world, even those who were progressives and always talking about how 'silence isn't spiritual,' were just…silent," she said. "I got the hate letters saying, 'Hope what you've done to [him] happens to you tenfold' and 'I hope you die.'"[13]

We vilify the survivor and rush to affirm the accused—to our peril. In the aftermath of the celebrity pastor scandal, the ax's cut was swift— all the elders and both teaching pastors (meant to replace him in retirement) stepped down. Those who touted the importance of leadership had a massive failure of actual leadership on their hands—all of which could have been avoided had the leaders chosen to slow down, listen, hire an impartial external investigator, and attempt to do the right thing. When churches circle the wagons, survivors get pummeled.

There is a place for righteous anger in the church. We *should* be angry that sexual abuse is occurring. We *should* be angry that people are being harmed both by predation and our anemic, victim-blaming response. Some of my greatest moments of healing came when someone else simply became enraged over the injustice I suffered. Properly placed, anger can be a powerful tool to enact change in the church.

DON'T DEMAND FORGIVENESS

We need to trust the journey the Holy Spirit has for a sexual abuse survivor and avoid prescribing their forgiveness journey. Counselor Chuck Roberts writes:

I would advise churches to respond with compassion, first and foremost. It seems to me they often start with trying to determine if it's really true. They should educate themselves on the matter and understand it is extremely rare for someone to falsely claim sexual abuse. I mean, who wants that to be their story? Then they often move on to trying to rush the victim to forgive their abuser. Stop! Forgiveness is a process that cannot be forced or rushed. And don't confuse forgiveness with reconciliation.[14]

Jimmy Hinton challenges the way we've been taught about forgiveness. As a pastor, he asked his congregation "how many of them have ever heard that forgiveness is for their own sake and *not* for their abuser or the person who sinned against them." He goes on:

Nearly every hand went up. Then I asked how many of them actually experienced *increased* anxiety and ongoing inner turmoil as a result of putting that principle into practice. All but three or four hands went up. We blindly tell people that forgiving the person who wronged them is for the victim's own sake (a concept that I have yet to find in the Holy Scriptures) and that they must forgive their abuser even if the abuser is unrepentant. Ironically, at least in my own congregation, that instead created confusion and actually *increased* their level of anxiety.[15]

Forgiveness is, of course, a central tenet of the Christian life. Because of what Jesus did on the cross, we, who have sinned often against a holy God, have complete access to him through Jesus. We live as a forgiven people. But how do we become forgiven in the first place? By asking God to forgive us. By repenting before him, telling him we're sorry. To repent means to turn away from sin, to forsake it for the sake of following the narrow road of salvation. It means to acknowledge our sin in the light, vowing to change our ways. If we never did this, if we just expected God to convey forgiveness without our demonstrated repentance, then every human being on earth would be walking around forgiven. That's the essence of what Bonhoeffer calls "cheap grace"—all the benefits of a forgiven life without not only any acknowledgment of sin but a stated desire to continue brashly in that sin, come what may.

But how does this apply to our relationships? What happens when someone who has harmed us doesn't ask for forgiveness? Consider Luke 17:3-4, noting the word "if": "So watch yourselves! If another believer sins, rebuke that person; then if there is repentance, forgive. Even if that person wrongs you seven times a day and each time turns again and asks forgiveness, you must forgive." What precedes forgiveness? Repentance and asking for forgiveness. Most often sexual predators do not repent of their ways; seldom do they ask for forgiveness. While it is important to forsake a bitter heart while letting go of the pain a perpetrator caused, that process is wholly individual. And really, only God knows the state of a survivor's heart enough to even know where they are on that relinquishment journey. To force-prescribe forgiveness on a traumatized person is to superimpose your perceived road of recovery over them, forsaking the fact that God has each on a unique journey. It's to take the place of God in their lives.

Forgiveness, after a survivor works through the complicated layers of it, doesn't negate justice. And the first step toward justice comes when the one who harmed awakens to the pain they've caused—both to the One who created them and the one they violated.

Looking at the life of Joseph in Genesis, we see this dual violation. His brothers trafficked him, never spending a moment searching for him after they sold him into slavery, allowing their father to believe he'd died—an affront to both Joseph and to the God who created him. Joseph spends many years working through the trauma of violent betrayal, coming to a place of prominence in Egypt after many trials. Yet he weeps when he sees his brothers for the first time after they come to Egypt to buy grain during the famine, still traumatized. The brothers seem to live unharmed lives after their treachery with the exception that they, too, were experiencing the plight of famine.

Eventually, his brothers understood the great sin they committed against their brother and God. In Genesis 42:21, after Joseph angrily imprisons his brothers during their first visit, they said, "Clearly we are being punished because of what we did to Joseph long ago. We saw his anguish when he pleaded for his life, but we wouldn't listen. That's why we're in this trouble." In Genesis 44:16 after they'd been "caught" with all their money during the second trip, Judah says, "God is punishing us for our sins." All this back and forth between Joseph and his brothers causes their pushed-down regret to finally surface. They're exposed. And it's only after their sin declaration that Joseph reveals himself through tears. Acknowledgment of their sin preceded restored relationship. Justice, where Joseph's brothers finally realize their guilt, begins when the truth is revealed.

The story doesn't end with vengeance, however. Revenge, we're taught in Romans 12:19, is God's territory, not ours: "Dear friends, never take revenge. Leave that to the righteous anger of God. For the Scriptures say, 'I will take revenge; I will pay them back,' says the LORD." Here Paul quotes a passage Joseph would remember: Deuteronomy 32:35. And as the truth is laid bare before them, we see Joseph's now-merciful heart emerge. Whereas he pushed his brothers to confess during their back-and-forth journeys, at the end of Genesis, we see a new dynamic. When Jacob dies, Joseph's brothers worry about the vengeance Joseph might take, so they tell him a lie, saying their father told them to ask Joseph to forgive them "for their sin in treating you so cruelly" (50:17). Joseph's response reveals the fruit of his lengthy forgiveness journey: "But Joseph replied, 'Don't be afraid of me. Am I God, that I can punish you? You intended to harm me, but God intended it all for good. He brought me to this position so I could save the lives of many people. No, don't be afraid. I will continue to take care of you and your children.' So he reassured them by speaking kindly to them" (50:19-21).

Mercy was the benevolent by-product of truth, confession, and repentance, but so often we reverse the order, demanding mercy before anyone ever tells the truth, admits their sinful actions, and turns away. This type of demanding breeds confusion for sexual abuse survivors.

One survivor elaborated on those feelings of confusion and frustration:

> The whole forgiveness thing has me so confused and distorted. I've been told that I need to forgive my abuser and

myself. What am I forgiving myself for? I was fourteen. It makes me feel responsible when I hear that…It's easy to tell someone to forgive their abuser when they've not been abused by him. By forgiving him I feel like I'm enabling him.[16]

We must exercise caution in this area. It is best to leave the decision to forgive (which is a layered decision) to the survivor of the crime and the Spirit living within. We must remember the decades-long journey of Joseph, who didn't magically become an agent of mercy. We must remember, too, that Joseph was never blamed for his brothers' betrayal. Telling survivors they must repent and ask forgiveness for how they either invited the abuse or responded to it is pure evil.

APOLOGIZE WHEN NECESSARY

Similar to being honest, if there is something to apologize for, do it. If a church missed signs, it should own up to their mistakes. If a parent or caregiver failed to protect—even if they didn't see abuse in the moment—apologize. And even if blame is elusive, practice what Nehemiah did—a corporate repentance. He confessed sins he didn't commit (but his nation did): "I confess that we have sinned against you. Yes, even my own family and I have sinned!" (Nehemiah 1:6). We should humble ourselves and issue a similar confession on behalf of the systems, hierarchies, and leadership who failed to report crime, dignify survivors, or be agents of justice and mercy. Apologies should be deliberate and proactive and should include language that demonstrates a recognition of responsibility.

WELCOME INDEPENDENT INVESTIGATION

When something is amiss, hire an independent investigator—not a PR firm, not a lawyer deeply connected to the church or mission and paid for by the church, but a truly independent entity. Netgrace.org offers independent investigations and has helped many institutions deal redemptively with past indiscretions and failures of leadership.[17]

An independent investigation gives confidence to those within and outside the institution, knowing the investigation is not tainted by affinity, bias, nepotism, or protectionism. Belmont Church, a 100-plus-year-old church in Nashville, Tennessee, has done something unheard-of. They've chosen to hire an independent investigator to look for abuses they aren't yet aware of. "We knew we needed someone who can see things objectively, to make sure we're doing this the right way. The Church in America has been so afraid of 'being attacked' by our culture that we cover up anything that doesn't make us look good."[18]

REPORT ABUSE

If a pastor harmed others, fire him or her. Try to get perpetrators the help they need—intensive therapy, etc., but do not let them continue in their position. Like wolves lurking near a flock of sheep, they must be removed no matter what the fallout. Safety and justice are more important than the reputation of the abuser.

But simply removing the abuser is not enough. Churches are not equipped to investigate crimes or verify the validity of a survivor's claims. They are not able to provide justice or understand the scope of the crime. If someone discloses abuse, report it to the police immediately. Let the legal system do what they're equipped to do. Encourage the survivor to get help via professional services and counseling. But don't try to be the police, an investigator, a lawyer, or a counselor.

PROVIDE FOR SURVIVORS

If a leader has harmed one of your congregants, choose to provide for survivors. Don't just set aside hush-hush money in order to settle out of court, but use resources for empowering the survivor in trauma-informed counseling and community resources. Not only that, but make a public commitment to radically dignify those who have dared to speak out.

CREATE CHILD PROTECTION POLICIES AND PROCEDURES

Every church should have child protection policies and procedures. And not only that, but these policies should also be revisited, revised, and reviewed frequently with staff. It's not enough to simply create a manual. The policies must be actively put into place. Sadly, many churches fall back on dated rules in order to "save" them from litigation. Having cameras in every room is a good safeguard, but should not be the reason we let our guards down. Many perpetrators know camera blind spots. Having two adults in a room with children at all times also is important, but provides a false sense of security. Policies are important, yes, but continual education and practice is the true measure of a proactive church.

Here are some elements of good safety procedures:

- Education: The church not only educates workers, but also provides education, even from the pulpit, about the dangers and stealthy practices of perpetrators. These would be regularly scheduled meetings and trainings. GRACE offers training like this—both for the congregation and those who work with children.[19]

- Stated Policies: How, exactly, will children be protected? What are the bathroom rules? Will there be cameras in rooms? How are children checked in and checked out to prevent abduction? How are leaders selected? How often are these policies taught and retaught to teachers and workers? What are expected safe behaviors of workers? How would a leader respond to a child's abuse disclosure? What are the penalties if an adult or teen worker violates protocol?

- Committee: Does the church have a child safeguarding committee who will oversee the implementation of the policies as well as a continuation of education?

- Timelines: What exactly will a church do when an allegation is disclosed? This must include reporting abuse, communicating honestly about it, finding help for survivors, and continued support of anyone harmed. Members should know the chain of command in how to approach an abuse allegation.

- Background Checks: Abuse will most likely happen—either within the church, or certainly outside the church doors. Its inevitability means we must at the least state that we will engage in vigorous background checks.[20] Not all offenders have records, but there are ways to dig deeper. Expanding the criminal check beyond local to the state and federal level helps. Also confirm a person's education, checking state and federal sex offender registries, and examining motor vehicle records as well as professional boards to see if there have been any violations recorded there. Also, a surprising amount of information can be discovered by sifting through a candidate's social media posts. Asking for references several layers deep, then actually following up with them, can reveal information that a clean background check cannot. One church nearly hired a youth pastor with a stellar resumé and no legal problems. However, after calling references, they discovered the applicant had an inappropriate relationship with a minor.[21]

- Proactive Policies for Existing Sex Offenders: We need to have written policies about what a church will do to address sex offenders in their midst.[22] Will they be allowed to worship alongside others? Will they have access to children?[23]

For more information, simply check out *The Child Safeguarding Policy Guide for Churches and Ministries* by Basyle Tchividjian and Shira M. Berkovits. They offer clear guidelines, an underlying philosophy of protection, and sample policies and worksheets for churches to be successful in this endeavor.

CHASE THE NOW-AND-NOT-YET KINGDOM

Sexual abuse is always an abuse of power—of one person exercising their power over another. In order to move through healing in a redemptive manner, we must have a robust understanding of the upside-down power dynamic of the kingdom. Worldly power invites collusion, control, and corruption, but the kingdom is about laying down rights, seeking the prosperity of the broken, and giving voice to the voiceless. Jesus ushered in this kingdom, and he exemplified it by his life, not lording his authority over others, and certainly not by overthrowing the Roman Empire. He served. He ran from power. He bent to the lowest place and washed the dusty roads of Palestine from the feet of his disciples. We represent this upside-down kingdom as we creatively imagine the coming kingdom where no tears, predation, or violence happens. In the kingdom of the new heavens and the new earth, sexual violence will not exist, so when we work to eradicate it, we reveal that aspirational kingdom today.

WELCOME PUBLIC STORIES

Whether a pastor has a personal story of abuse or people in the congregation are given the platform to share their journeys, finding ways to highlight stories enables people in the pews to feel emboldened and no longer alone. Too often we've created a culture of perfection in our churches with a facade of people with no substantive problems. If we want to be truly relevant and effectual, we'll begin to build a community of the broken on the back of well-told stories.

My friend Boz recounted a beautiful example of how simply sharing a story can change a community. Heidi Hankel is a Presbyterian pastor and abuse survivor. A year before she was called to a congregation of 85 people, a man in the church had been arrested and prosecuted for sexual abuse. She found it puzzling that no one talked about it, as if the abuse never occurred. In response, she chose to preach a multipart sermon series on abuse to the older congregation. She was surprised at what happened next. After the sermon series, 25 women confided in her about their own stories of abuse—nearly a third of the congregation! The women ranged in age from 60 to 85—some coming forward for the very first time. Imagine living seven decades with a secret! These folks never felt safe until Pastor Hankel gave permission by going first. In doing so, she created a safe place for 25 people.[24]

PRAY

Make space to pray for abuse survivors. Bent Tree Bible Fellowship in North Texas creates pockets of time for prayer at the end of some sermons, giving people permission to bring their grief to others for prayer. While there can be abuse with prayer, particularly when we rely on formulas to fix others ("just pray this prayer and all will be well"), there is also great power in acknowledging that we're out of our league in trying to heal. We need God. We need his intervention and tender compassion. We need to know he is interested in our plight. So much of my own healing came on the heels of other people daring to pray for me.

GIVE GRACE SPACE

We must create an atmosphere of grace in our churches, coupled with a dynamic view of the church. Sometimes people are so harmed in one church that they have to move on. That's okay. Allow for that kind of redemptive movement. Doug writes:

> Releasing expectations and serving people is an expression of love. The goal is not to get things back to "normal" but to serve the wounded person as they pursue a new way of being in the world. The church holds such powerful memories, that it can be incredibly difficult for someone to stay in that church after the relationship has fractured. Consequently, both abuser and the abused sometimes leave. It is important to accept people who make this difficult decision. To relationally help with transitions and to remind them that faith and the kingdom are far bigger than the building they feel they can no longer enter. There are so many complicated issues and we must be full of kindness, grace and acceptance as people navigate their pain.

Sometimes building the church means letting people go, understanding that the church is all of us, worshipping in different locales. No single local church is "the" church. We are all the body of Christ.

LIFT THE MAZE

In an article entitled "God of the Second Shift," Jeff Haanen recounts the story of Doug Muder, whose father was a laborer. He makes the point that, vocationally speaking, some of us, through no fault of our own, are placed at the entrance of the maze because of difficult circumstances, economic distress, or prejudice, while others are placed near its exit. Those at the back of the maze have to make every single correct turn to make it to the end, while those who are advantaged simply have to make a few good choices. "Now, imagine that you're overlooking the maze and you have compassion for those still inside. You ask questions like 'Couldn't we knock out a few walls?'"[25] Or better yet, why don't we lift the maze entirely, allowing everyone to move freely?

Those who have experienced abuse often feel like the journey is fraught with obstacles and dead ends, while those who haven't walked through abuse don't understand why they can't "get over it and move on." Seeing the maze gives people empathy for those farther back, and lifting it gives survivors hope. We lift the maze by giving voice to people's stories that differ from ours. We lift it again by actively listening without judgment. We lift it through face-to-face conversations. And all this happens when church leadership chooses to go first and model this kind of learner's posture, showing that hierarchies between people are not kingdom constructs.

WELCOME EVERYONE TO THE TABLE

Perhaps the most powerful thing we can do is to welcome all kinds of voices to the table—inviting people of color, immigrants, the economically disadvantaged, the aging, and women to the discourse, giving them positions of leadership. Otherwise, our theology and praxis (the way we live out our theology) will be limited to one narrow perspective.

Part of our current crisis is that, for the most part, the male perspective has dominated church leadership. Whatever you think about women in leadership, both perspectives will benefit from women having a voice. My counselor friend Chuck agrees: "Get more women in leadership! It doesn't mean mistakes will never happen, but women bring a needed voice and wisdom that we're foolish to leave out of leadership."[26]

Beth Moore has taken flak for speaking about the need for more women in spheres of influence. And when she does, she's met with evangelical ire—but not in the way you'd expect. When she writes about the problem of misogyny, it's not necessarily the anger of men that surprised her, it's the pushback she receives from other women, some who declared they'd never read another one of her Bible studies. Nevertheless, she persists. "While Moore was devastated by what she had allowed herself to see in the institution for which she had so much love and respect, she was undeterred by the criticism coming her way."[27]

Women make up the majority of North American congregations. They do the lion's share of work around the local church. Surely, giving them more voice would only *benefit* the church, particularly in protecting people from abuse. We need their perspective.

Pre-fall, we see a beautiful mutuality in Adam and Eve, a tandem leadership fleshed out in the Garden of Eden. Post-fall, we experienced the fallout of sin, particularly in male-female relationships. Now, however, we live in the age of grace, where Jesus has birthed a return to Eden, saving us from ourselves. Paul reminds us that we are all one, no longer divided into hierarchies: "There is no longer Jew or Gentile, slave or free, male and female. For you are all one in Christ Jesus" (Galatians 3:28). We look forward to the day when every knee will bow (men, women, slaves, free, all denominations, all skin colors) before the throne. There is no hierarchy among those who bow; we are all equally submitted to our true, tender authority: Jesus. This kind of humility should inform whom we welcome into leadership. If earth is our preparation for heaven, why not empower all who will eventually worship before the throne?

ACCOUNT OF A FAILURE OF LEADERSHIP

Jules Woodson, whose youth pastor assaulted her on a backcountry road, has an important perspective on what her church should have done. Her quote is long, but I believe her voice is prophetic. She writes, "There are multiple things that I would have liked to see happen when I first reported my abuse." She goes on to detail what could have been done differently:

- First, I really wish I had not been blamed. As soon as I heard, "So you're telling me you participated?" I immediately started to feel as if I had done something wrong and therefore was to blame. In an instant, I felt completely alone.

- Second, I wish that I had received love, encouragement, and support. Never once was I offered any sort of help, not from the staff or anyone else. I was never asked about what I needed, and I certainly was not given any options for how to proceed. The only "advice" I ever got was that I was to never speak to him again, and that I shouldn't talk about what happened with anyone else.

- Third, I wish they would have taken my allegations seriously and pulled him off staff immediately. They saw what happened as only a sin, not a crime. They allowed him to go on, as if nothing had happened…He even went on to teach a weekend of True Love Waits to the youth group! It wasn't until weeks later, when I told the girls in my discipleship group that I was struggling and why, that church leadership finally pulled him from his position. Had I not told more people, I don't think they would have ever done anything.

- Fourth, I wish they would have been honest with the congregation that my former youth pastor had sexually abused a minor in the youth group. This would have been important for several reasons to include, allowing any other potential victims a safe place to come forward, halting any rumors that were starting to spread, and showing the congregation that they take reports of crimes seriously and as pastors, they have a zero tolerance policy when it comes to leaders abusing their authority.

- Last and most importantly, I wish they had immediately called the police and reported what I had told them. At age 17, and after being traumatized by the sexual assault, I didn't have the slightest clue about what to do, much less did I understand that I had the option of talking to law enforcement.

Years later, when Jules discovered that her former youth pastor became a staff pastor of a popular megachurch, she again experienced a strange, ill-informed reaction. She writes,

> There are several ways the church could have responded differently this year. Let me preface this by telling you that I found out along with the rest of the world, that Sunday after I went public with my story, that the lead pastor had known that he sexually assaulted a minor in his youth group back in Texas, but hired him anyway and never reported the abuse. This information was shocking as well as devastating.

She believes:

- The former youth pastor should have been suspended from his position as soon as they were made aware of my story, and indefinitely until they could get the results of an independent third party investigation.

- That as soon as the church knew, either that the lead pastor would stand behind the man who abused me 100 percent, or that he had known about the abuse all along, he should have been immediately suspended, pending an investigation.

- That the church definitely should have never given either
  of them a platform to speak. Allowing them to go on stage
  and minimize what happened to me, preach about casting stones, say they were saddened that I had not been
  on the same road to healing, and ultimately be celebrated
  with a standing ovation, was not only traumatizing to
  me but potentially any other victim who watched what
  happened.[28]

The saddest part of her story is the missed opportunity to display
the love of Jesus to the world. She writes,

> The church missed a great opportunity to demonstrate, as
> Jesus often did, that it should be the safest place for the
> wounded and the vulnerable. They had a chance to show
> the world that the church will absolutely not tolerate a
> shepherd who abuses one of his flock nor anyone who cov-
> ers for that person. Their blatant disregard to show empa-
> thy and integrity when confronted, not only with my story
> of clergy sexual abuse by their now pastor, but the subse-
> quent emotional and spiritual abuse I endured in connec-
> tion with reporting my abuse 20 years ago to my pastor,
> shows the world just how much the church still has yet to
> learn regarding abuse and trauma.

LISTEN TO JENNIFER

My friend Jennifer is one of my favorite people. She thinks differently, loves extravagantly, and lives winsomely in the aftermath of
abuse. Her advice to the church makes me want to sing in freedom.
Her advice:

- You aren't there to do public relations for God, so instead
  of spinning the story for Jesus, try to actually listen, empathize, mourn, ache, and feel with those who are victimized.

- Remember Job's friends, and don't try to tell someone why
  their suffering happened because that never ends well.

- The "God never gives us more than we can handle" line is as callous as it is unbiblical, so trash it.

- Basically find a way to sit in your discomfort, and don't try to minimize or tidy it up or fix it so that everyone can "move on."

- Don't make someone who has been spiritually eviscerated apologize for bleeding on your carpet.

- Don't hijack their story by making their pain about your experience with it.

- Try not to be so squeamish and delicate. Toughen up and be a support. Don't gasp and swoon like this person has just blown up your bleach-bright bubble with their dirty trauma.

- The real Jesus is big enough and strong enough to hang with this kind of stuff, so no need to bring a shiny plastic one in to substitute. If you don't have access to that Jesus, sit out this kind of work and hot-potato it to someone who does.

The task before us looms large, but I believe it's not impossible. Returning to a New Testament understanding of church and an old-fashioned shepherding perspective isn't flashy, but it's effective. The late Eugene Peterson laments our departure from truly shepherding people: "We've lost a talent for relations and showing interest in the other person. We don't have community because we skip over the critical part: being in relationship with the people, knowing their kids, knowing the neighborhood."[29] Perhaps that perspective informed his translation of John 1:14: "The Word became flesh and blood, and moved into the neighborhood. We saw the glory with our own eyes, the one-of-a-kind glory, like Father, like Son, Generous inside and out, true from start to finish." We must live this truth—Jesus moving into our traumatized neighborhoods. He is the One who teaches us empathy, justice, and hope. He demonstrated how to listen. He valued the voices of outcasts, foreigners, and women. He healed humanity when he touched them, one by one. That, too, is our mission.

CHAPTER TWELVE

A PROPHETIC IMAGINATION

I say let the stories come. Let them all come out. This wickedness so transcends our normal divides that the "whataboutism" game we play has become laughable. No matter your tribe, your tribe is guilty. So let every attempt to deflect or defend come to an end, and let us instead listen and learn from the courage of the abused. They are our prophets now, with voices that will no longer allow us to hide or ignore the epidemic. Indeed, the long overdue purge has begun, and may it not relent until every hidden darkness faces the light of justice.

ROBERT CUNNINGHAM[1]

We stand on the cusp of revival. People are fed up with secrecy, covering up, and the sheer proliferation of abuse—both inside and outside the church. The anger fueled by the #MeToo and #ChuchToo movements is tangible and shows no sign of relenting. People are finding their vocal chords, and reform is burgeoning from the groundswell. All great movements of history are fueled by anger at injustice. Abolition, labor reform, the right to vote, child welfare, the civil rights movement—all started with a kernel of anger toward something people perceived to be wholly unjust. In most every case, people came to this conclusion because of the power of story—*even* when it didn't personally affect them. We see this in *Uncle Tom's Cabin* in the case of slavery in the USA, or Upton Sinclair's *The Jungle* in the case of labor laws and meatpacking safety. The pattern emerges: Story fuels anger; anger fuels reform.

Today another flood of stories has crossed our collective transoms.

If we harness this story-fueled movement, rather than push against it, we will experience a necessary reformation. No longer will the church tolerate and protect abusers, but it will be a haven for the broken. No longer will we stand on the sidelines and resign ourselves to the fact that this is just how the world works—predatory people allowed to abuse unchecked and unhindered. No more. As the popular hashtag reminds us, #SilenceIsNotSpiritual. But advocacy is.

It is time for a prophetic imagining of what the church can and should be: a place of security, not shame; humbleness, not pride— a place where we follow the radical steps of the One who took our place, served us well, and sacrificed everything for us. If we simply follow the Golden Rule and do unto others who have been sexually harmed as we would prefer to be treated, revival can't help but burst out. When we consider a prophetic imagination of what could be, we simply need to turn backward in our Bibles toward the prophets who also possessed this kind of future hope.

REVIVAL FOR THE CHURCH

In Isaiah 58, we see the nation of Israel in a state similar to that of the modern church. Israel is piously going through the motions of religiosity, yet failing to help others. You can hear the agony in God's voice as, through Isaiah, he tries to lift their vision for what could be:

> Shout with the voice of a trumpet blast. Shout aloud! Don't be timid. Tell my people Israel of their sins! Yet they act so pious! They come to the Temple every day and seem delighted to learn all about me. They act like a righteous nation that would never abandon the laws of its God. They ask me to take action on their behalf, pretending they want to be near me (Isaiah 58:1-2).

Here bows a "pious" people who are all about the perception of holiness. In these pleas, you hear echoes of Jesus's discourses with the Pharisees, those he referred to as filthy cups and whitewashed tombs (see Matthew 23:25-28).

Apparently, Israel continued the facade of piety by fasting. They asked God indignantly, *Why haven't you noticed our sacrifice?* He reminds them that words matter less than actions, and actions focused on looking good have nothing to do with his heart for people:

> No, this is the kind of fasting I want: Free those who are wrongly imprisoned; lighten the burden of those who work for you. Let the oppressed go free, and remove the chains that bind people. Share your food with the hungry, and give shelter to the homeless. Give clothes to those who need them, and do not hide from relatives who need your help (Isaiah 58:6-7).

God instructs the nation of Israel on what James later declared to Christ followers: Faith without compassionate works is just words (see James 2:14-26). We see this type of loving action present in the first-century church, where believers cared for one another in small communities, sacrificing for each other joyfully.

If the great and glorious chosen ones rouse themselves through true repentance and righteous action, God promises light and hope and beauty. Just look at the promises in Isaiah 58:8-14 for those who take seriously the mandate to love people well:

- Our salvation will come like the dawn.
- Our wounds will quickly heal.
- Our godliness will lead us forward.
- God's glory will protect us from behind.
- God will hear us.
- Our light will shine out in the darkness.
- The darkness will become as the light of noon.
- God will guide us continually.
- He will give us water.
- He will restore our strength.
- We will become like a well-watered garden.

- We will be like ever-flowing springs.
- We will rebuild the ruins of our cities.
- We will be known as the rebuilder of protective walls.
- We will become a restorer of homes.
- God will become our great delight.
- He will honor us.
- He will grant us an inheritance.

The church acts most like Jesus when it protects the victimized. We should be known as builders of protective walls. Sadly, we *have* built walls, but those walls have protected the institution of the church out of fear. No more. Please, no more.

The grand narrative of Scripture is the story of a rebellious people who harm each other while their powerful triune God risked everything to reconcile them to himself. And this God has given us a mandate, beautifully stated in 2 Corinthians 5:19-21:

> For God was in Christ, reconciling the world to himself, no longer counting people's sins against them. And he gave us this wonderful message of reconciliation. So we are Christ's ambassadors; God is making his appeal through us. We speak for Christ when we plead, "Come back to God!" For God made Christ, who never sinned, to be the offering for our sin, so that we could be made right with God through Christ.

We are his ambassadors, beckoning a broken world to the Broken One. As the body of Christ, we represent Jesus on this earth. It may seem simplistic to ask the same old question, "What would Jesus do?" but that is the kind of simplicity on which revivals are built.

- How would Jesus treat a sexual abuse survivor?
- If Jesus discovered a pastor in a church who abused children, how would he react?
- Would Jesus care more for the reputation of a local church or a bleeding stranger in front of him?

What would Jesus do? He would listen, intercede, and care for the broken. He would fashion a whip out of cords and chastise the church for preferring protection of itself (and its economic viability) to the protection and restoration of survivors. But, sadly, we've lost sight of this very real Jesus—in our institutions, famous ministries, or human-built structures. We are concerned more for our glory than his. We've become unwitting idolaters, worshipping what we create more than we worship the crucified and risen One who always dignified the marginalized. If we truly worship Jesus, we will love those who suffer. We will care for the needs of the hurting. We will be both Good Samaritans *and* good shepherds.

A MIGHTY RIVER

This summer, while listening to the radio, I heard the story of a woman recovering from a stroke. She used to be in the US military in Afghanistan, and, while there, engaged with local people. She found poetry to be a beautiful entry point for understanding and conversation. Post-stroke, she is struggling to regain her language. She consoles herself with an Afghani proverb, *Qatra qatra darya maisha*—"A river is made drop by drop."[2]

The pathway of justice for abuse survivors feels a lot like recovering language after a stroke: slogged, laborious, and frustrating. Imagining the river of justice can either encourage or discourage. It can encourage because we know the drops are building toward something. It can discourage because we know how long it takes for drops to build into streams, currents, and rivers. In our instantaneous culture, we want to "social media" a quick, painless solution, yet great movements of history sometimes slog. Couple that with how instant media fuels compassion fatigue (because of the sheer volume of the stories), and you see how discouragement can overcome a person. That happened to me. After battling a heavy weight of sadness after hearing more stories of predation recounted by strangers and people I know, I had to take a break from it all, refraining from predator stories, waiting on God for rejuvenation. I pulled away to process my grief with good friends. I took long walks in the woods. I smiled when I read my daughter Julia's text from work: "This drunk guy was talking about how the #MeToo movement is a bunch of [lies], and it took every part of my being to not yell at him. I wanted to say, 'My mom is writing a book about people like you who doubt survivors.' But I didn't want to get fired." Julia's twentysomething generation gives me hope.

Why? Because the drops seem to be moving from trickle to stream.

Holy momentum is rushing forward in the generations that follow.

We've heard the prophetic imagination of Isaiah, but now I'd like to turn us toward Amos. His words are poignant, especially as churches, missions organizations, and Christian establishments have, in the past, tried desperately to dam up the trickle of healing. By their silence, their hushing, and their choice to handle things in-house for the sake of their public image, they have denied justice to survivors of abuse. They resemble the idolatrous nation of Israel as God speaks these words over them:

> With blinding speed and power he destroys the strong, crushing all their defenses. *How you hate honest judges! How you despise people who tell the truth!* You trample the poor, stealing their grain through taxes and unfair rent. Therefore, though you build beautiful stone houses, you will never live in them. Though you plant lush vineyards, you will never drink wine from them. For I know the vast number of your sins and the depth of your rebellions. You oppress good people by taking bribes and deprive the poor of justice in the courts. So those who are smart keep their mouths shut, for it is an evil time. Do what is good and run from evil so that you may live! Then the Lord God of Heaven's Armies will be your helper, just as you have claimed. *Hate evil and love what is good; turn your courts into true halls of justice.* Perhaps even yet the Lord God of Heaven's Armies will have mercy on the remnant of his people (Amos 5:9-15, emphasis mine).

Truth and justice matter to our Creator.

We live in a similar time as Amos, but in our era, it's been ministries and churches in the name of Jesus who deny justice for those preyed upon. The tide, though, is turning. I believe my little raindrop and your tiny rivulet and her trickle are, drop by drop, becoming a mighty river of justice. I am not naive; I know perfect justice does not exist on this earth. But I do know that one day all things will be made right as hearts are laid bare before his holy gaze. But in the in-between time, between the now and the not yet, God gives us the privilege to be his salt and light in this world. He empowers us to be his emissaries of truth-telling, grace-giving, winsome storytelling.

We tell our stories, and a drop of truth lands on the dry ground. The ground sings back. Alone, that would be the conclusion to the story—dry ground absorbing one small raindrop. But another story is told, and another drop wets the ground. And another. Then another. And slowly, beautifully, powerfully, the stories carve a pathway through, and that pathway becomes a trickle where others with painful stories refresh themselves. Before long, this trickle becomes a stream that heals the nations. And soon it is a powerful river of justice.

We see this phenomenon toward the end of Amos 5. God wants to clean Israel of religious hypocrisy and align it with his character, which has always been to watch over the oppressed. Let these words terrify and encourage you, church.

> I hate all your show and pretense—the hypocrisy of your religious festivals and solemn assemblies. I will not accept your burnt offerings and grain offerings. I won't even notice all your choice peace offerings. Away with your noisy hymns of praise! I will not listen to the music of your harps. Instead, I want to see a mighty flood of justice, an endless river of righteous living (Amos 5:21-24).

Drop by drop, friends. Little by little. Story by story. What does this mean for the postmodern church? It means honesty from the pulpit—where survivor stories are given teeth and platform. It means less emphasis on bigger is better and more on community discipleship and greater spiritual growth (things that are hard to measure). It means exposing hypocrisy, even if it means risking corporate reputation. It means repenting of sin, starting with leaders. It means practicing peace with others by listening, truly hearing, and taking a learner's posture—even when the conversation veers toward uncomfortable. It means not merely singing platitudes about how brave and amazing we are, but whisper-singing praise to the great and awesome God we serve. His glory, not ours. His fame, not ours. His reputation, not ours. His power, not ours. It means we will long more for justice than what appears conveniently judicious at the time. It means embodying the words of Proverbs 11:25: "The generous will prosper; those who refresh others will themselves be refreshed."

For those of you wearied from watering the dry ground: Don't give up. Your drop is not inconsequential; it is vital.

The river foams.

When we walk into a church, we want to know it's a place of truth. Of light. Of honesty. We want to know that it's a safe place, particularly for the most vulnerable. But no place is safe that harbors secrets in the dark. No place is safe as long as perpetrators are allowed to flourish.

Imagine two churches with me. One church—let's call it Church A—covers up sexual abuse, quietly allows for a perpetrator to move to another congregation without even a warning and certainly no legal action, then maligns survivors into silence. The congregation is blessedly unaware, and the shiny reputation of the church remains intact. Financial giving is up. Leaders stay in power. Confirmation bias is confirmed.

Another church—Church B—exposes sexual abuse, reports the perpetrator to law enforcement, sets up emergency counseling, and offers long-term care to survivors. This church speaks openly about what happened with tears and repentance for any part they played. The congregation is educated on the dynamics of abuse, grieves the loss of innocence, yet learns to trust a leadership that isn't afraid to do the right thing. The church's reputation, amazingly, remains intact because of their integrity in handling the situation. The church itself isn't as concerned about tithes or power. The leadership is consumed with loving and serving the flock and its ongoing needs. Confirmation bias is gone. Truth flourishes. In fact, more survivors of other past abuses come forward, tell their stories for the first time, get counseling, and begin to minister to the countless people in their community also affected by sexual abuse. The church becomes a haven. Reputation doesn't grow because of fancy image campaigns, slick branding, or perfectly crafted statements that place the blame elsewhere. Reputation grows by word of mouth, a groundswell of admiration and awe, much like what happened in the book of Acts (see 2:42-47).

Church A reminds me of John's warning: "The world offers only a craving for physical pleasure, a craving for everything we see, and pride in our achievements and possessions. These are not from the Father, but are from this world" (1 John 2:16). This church is not a place of reality, but unreality. It prefers power over truth, wealth and reputation and fame more than doing the right thing.

Church B is a church I would trust more easily. Though no institution can do things perfectly (who can?), its desire to listen to survivors, obey the law, and provide transparency makes me have confidence in their humble leadership.

I'm not sure what class in seminary asserts that Church A's way is the preferable one. My hunch is that this idea of reputation management is woven into us, all because of fear. But here's the truth: God can handle his reputation just fine. He does not need a public relations firm or fearful leaders controlling narratives. He doesn't get glory when leaders cover up sin in the church. In fact, he instructs us to expose the sin. Paul told the Ephesians, "Take no part in the unfruitful works of darkness, but instead expose them" (5:11 ESV), and he exhorted the Corinthian church quite boldly to expose a deplorable sin (see 1 Corinthians 5:1-5). Reputation always thrives in truth—even when the truth hurts—never in hiding or covering up reality.

In Matthew 18:12-14 (NIV), Jesus asks,

> What do you think? If a man owns a hundred sheep, and one of them wanders away, will he not leave the ninety-nine on the hills and go to look for the one that wandered off? And if he finds it, truly I tell you, he is happier about that one sheep than about the ninety-nine that did not wander off. In the same way your Father in heaven is not willing that any of these little ones should perish.

I fear there are hundreds of thousands of sheep that have lost their way because of the sexual abuse crisis. Church leadership has silenced them. Especially when survivors report a church member or leader's deed to the proper authorities, only to be quieted, shamed, or ridiculed. Or they simply disclosed their story to a church member or leader (when abuse is unrelated to the church) and were met with silence or platitudes. In neither case is justice served. Perpetrators lived free without repercussion, while the deluge of triggers and shame and nightmares and PTSD symptoms continued on and on and on. So few leaders choose to leave the 99 to chase after the one victimized. Instead, we have chased the wolf, coddled it, kept it near, and given it a platform to tear into the remaining 99. This should not be. Jesus chased the lost sheep. We should do the same.

Our prophetic imagination is informed by what has happened in Scripture, and it is sparked in the present as the kingdom of God advances. But our hopes are most stirred by the promise of what is yet to come—the new heavens and the new earth, where every tear of every survivor is wiped away, and we will finally live whole and in harmony. It is this eschatological vision that propels us forward to love the broken. Chasing after the one sheep is our beautiful privilege. N.T. Wright eloquently reminds us of our blessed future:

> The New Testament invites us, then, to imagine a new world as a beautiful, healing community; to envisage it as a world vibrant with life and energy, incorruptible, beyond the reach of death and decay; to hold it in our mind's eye as a world reborn, set free from the slavery of corruption, free to be truly what it was made to be. This is the pole by which we must set our compasses so that we may find our way along the intermediate paths that lie before us.[3]

As we hold this future in our mind's eye, we work to see this kind of love and proactive sacrifice for all people—for our healing hearts, for our broken communities, and for his beautiful glory.

While the river rolls on.

THE LINGERING

I am the Alpha and the Omega,
the First and the Last,
the Beginning and the End.

REVELATION 22:13

I began this book in a doctor's office, and I will finish it on a cold Seattle beach. You've heard bits and pieces of my story throughout, particularly of the yearlong rapes at five—these all occurred in the Pacific Northwest in West Seattle, particularly Alki Beach. I had *never* returned to the scene of the crime—for over 40 years. But in 2016, I taught a writing intensive outside of Geneva, Switzerland, and met a lady named Glenda who would prove to change the course of my healing journey. There, I told my story as I always do (my abuse figures into my writing in many ways). She pulled me aside. "I want to help you locate the boys," she said.

At first, I dismissed her earnest offer, since I had not been able to uncover the mystery of their identity all these years, but her persistence won me over. She contacted her friend Nancy, who sacrificially agreed to go to the Seattle Public Library and do some sleuthing. Through the bits and pieces I was able to give her, including the first and last name of my babysitter, the location of my little white house, and the name of my elementary school and a nearby park, she found one of the boys. She uncovered that he had died in the 2000s of cancer, so I would not have to manage the decision of whether I would contact him or not. His house? Next door to the babysitter. And my house? A block and a half away. Everything as I remembered it began to snap into place. Since our family would go to Seattle that Christmas, Patrick and I decided that, after we said goodbye to our adult children, we would continue our journey to Alki.

I didn't sleep the night before we ventured to see all the places I'd avoided all those years. I jogged six miles in the workout room, sweating, fearing, trying to outrun my anxiety. My heart thumped, and I swallowed my reflux as we neared the area where evergreens stood tall and the sandy soil beckoned. But something beautiful happened when we parked in front of my excruciatingly *tiny* white house with peeling paint and a crooked picket fence. I felt a modicum of peace. I sat in the passenger's seat alive. The little white house, and the hell that existed within its neighborhood, had not slayed me. I opened the door, then inhaled the salt air, my breath an indication of life. I am still standing.

Yet, despite my stature, my heart grew sad. In that home, I had not been protected. I lived constantly afraid, battling nightmares, scary parties full of drug-using adults, and strangers who were both belligerent and indifferent toward me. I cannot remember the face of my stepfather, but I do remember the timbre of his yell. And though my mom lived there too, I have a hard time remembering her face in that locale. She seems more like a mist, a vapor untethered by the earth. It would have been her who washed my laundry, who would have seen the bloody evidence on my clothes. Yet she did nothing, asked nothing. She simply had not been curious.

We walked about a block and a half toward the beach in the crisp, evergreen air. I wondered if I would remember my babysitter's house, but the moment I saw it, everything rushed back in—the fear, loneliness, terror. As I stood before the two houses, I realized the power of proximity—a narrow sidewalk existed between the structures of the predator's home and the home of the one who allowed the preying. The nearness suddenly made a lot of sense. How convenient a target I was! A frightened girl harbored by an indifferent, evil caregiver who threw me away to those boys like garbage. We circled around to the alley behind Eva's house where I spied the door those perpetrators would politely knock on every day before they chose to rape me. Though still peaceful, something dark festered inside me, a niggling sense of horror that I could not shake. I dismissed it.

We walked to my elementary school—again, very close to my house. I told Patrick, "I know the dark and scary park is somehow connected to the school," but neither of us saw how. I began to doubt my recollection. Patrick snapped a picture of me smiling before the school—the place where my kindergarten teacher penalized me for acting out instead of investigating why a sweet, compliant child suddenly changed.

We found the park on a map and trekked in. This was not a happy park. Tall evergreens loomed skyward, blotting out the light, stealing my breath. I was five years old again, and these trees were the place of my degradation, standing like silent sentinels, swaying in the foggy air. Their bark had witnessed my betrayal, their indelible green, my horror. No swing sets. No laughing. Not even the bark of a dog punctuated the trails, ravines, and the heaviness of that setting. "This is a scary place, a dark place," Patrick said. I nodded.

"There," I said, pointing to one of the ravines. "See where we are on this trail? When the boys took me into the brambles below, I could see people walking above, and I longed for them to see me, to notice what was going on," I told Patrick. "But they muffled my cries with their hands." We said very little as the memories screamed into me. Everything, *everything* was how I remembered it. Every detail, including an obscured entrance to the park from the school. It had been connected, just as I remembered. Patrick snapped another picture, but my smile looks less genuine, more pasted.

In every location, we prayed. Patrick asked God for more healing, for closure, for freedom—my dear, interceding husband. I truly believe we heal better together. I prayed against the darkness. I tried to say goodbye to that memory-stained place. I hope I did. I certainly wanted to "end" this pain, to tie it up in a neat bow, complete with a victorious story.

We ended our quest by having lunch with the two sweet women who helped me figure all this out—in a restaurant by the beach. Then we headed by ferry to Vashon Island to celebrate our anniversary at a pristine spot overlooking the Puget Sound, where I hoped the lapping of waves, the enticement of a sunset, and the lingering quiet would salve the trauma I'd just endured. Again.

Shortly after I arrived, the vomiting began. I may have smiled, and my mind may have assented to my complete healing, but my body remembered. Violently. I vomited so much I feared I might need the hospital. Eventually, once our anniversary was over, my body stopped revolting against me, and I flew green-skinned back to Texas to face life again.

I share this not to gain empathy, but to remind us all that the trauma of sexual abuse is long and insidious. It wreaks havoc on the soul. It shapes how we perceive the world, our experience of God, the way we yell at ourselves in our heads. Trauma is the lifelong companion we never asked for, and it lingers far longer than we ever anticipated.

Because of the enduring legacy of that trauma, I wrote this book. I am a wounded healer who longs to see the church rise up into itself and do the unheralded, but necessary work of burden bearing. In so many ways, the church has been a blessing to me. Even this last story emphasizes that truth—Glenda's outrageous kindness, Nancy's decision to inconvenience herself by investigating for a stranger, my husband's empathetic prayers and presence. They are all the body of Christ being the hands and feet of Jesus to me. They embody the spirit of *We Too*.

We must tread tenderly on the soil of each other's stories, be empathetic as we listen, and simply determine to do the right thing.

Alki Beach will always frighten me. I'm not sure it's even wise to venture there again. But God, who has faithfully borne my burden, lives there too. He occupies all the difficult spaces humanity has endured. While I can't fully reconcile the problem of evil and why so many people have been sexually violated over the centuries, I do know this: Jesus has wept alongside me, and he weeps for his church to rise up valiantly and love the least, the last, and the lost. This is our *We Too* moment, to purposefully suffer alongside the sexually broken.

WE TOO MANIFESTO

W e understand that all human beings are made in the image of their Creator and, therefore, are worthy of protection and dignity. Because we understand the nefarious nature of predatory behavior, we value the voices of survivors over the bullying narrative of the abusers. Jesus sought the broken, the outcast, the sick, and the unnoticed, and we, as a church, continue that agape-fueled mission. We are willing to chase the one.

We understand that sexual abuse is the work of the evil one who came to steal, kill, and destroy humanity. We know that sexual abuse often causes lifelong traumatic results, healed in a multitude of ways, including therapy, prayer, compassionate listening, and simply walking alongside the hurting. In helping those who ache in the aftermath of abuse, we are determined to deal a debilitating blow to evil's proliferation.

We understand that sexual predation is not only an egregious sin, but it is also a crime. According to Romans 13, we honor the governing authorities in our nation, entrusting perpetrators to the judicial process. Instead of shrinking away in fear and covering up abuse when it's brought to light, we commit to alerting the appropriate institutions— law enforcement, mental health care, emergency services.

We know that the cry of the survivor is the church crying out. He

or she is us—and the level at which we deal redemptively and empathetically with the sexual abuse crisis corresponds directly to our ability to truly represent Jesus Christ on this earth. We commit to allowing
space for survivors to tell their stories in our churches. We welcome this
because healing comes through sharing.

The church is not a place of perfection. It is and should be a haven
of protection.

We are committed to protecting those children in our midst, and
we value this far more than the church's reputation. Given the choice
between protecting reputation and protecting children, we will always
choose the latter. We will create policies and procedures in our churches,
missions, and ministries that empower and protect those we serve. We
will declare that secrecy may have been the way past generations have
dealt with abuse, but that is not how we will address it today. We prefer light to darkness.

As believers in the good news of Jesus Christ, we declare that no
one is beyond his reach—even the perpetrator. But we will err on the
side of protection of the vulnerable in evaluating who can serve in our
churches, missions, and ministries.

We affirm this story: The blame rests on the shoulders of the one
who violated, not the one who was violated. We will not participate in
public or private victim-shaming, nor will we glory in the downfall of
the perpetrator. Instead, we purpose to pray for all involved as the legal
and therapeutic processes ensue. We also understand that God is glo-
rified when justice prevails.

We understand the church is in crisis. People have abandoned
church because we have not shepherded them. They leave because
their brokenness is treated with contempt, inconvenience, or dismissal.
They leave because they feel utterly alone in their stories because so few
abuse stories are even hinted at on Sunday mornings. While we long
to see the church grow deeper through discipleship and wider through
evangelism, instead we are experiencing a shameful exodus of the very
people who would offer the world the kind of authentic, raw hope
the next generation craves and needs. We are losing our clarion voice
because of our nearsighted fear of how messy we perceive the abused

can be. And yet, they are the ones Jesus pursued when he walked this earth and are the very people who can teach us to love the world Jesus died for. The sexually abused are our tutors, but we've expelled them. Now, we choose to welcome them.

We are collectively broken by the sheer volume of protectionism that has harmed victims over the years, decades, and millennia. So many silenced. So many secrets. So many people seemingly getting away with harming the vulnerable. We repent of our penchant for institutional protectionism. Instead of indifference, we choose active compassion. Instead of deafness, we choose to dignify people by listening to their stories. Instead of shrinking back in fear of the messiness of sexual assault, we choose to face the Goliaths of those churches and institutions that would rather dabble in reputation management than participate in righteous repentance. We grieve over all who have been harmed, silenced, shamed, and blamed. In repentance, we stand up for those who are silenced, unheard, maligned, mocked, and shut down with a holy tenacity to do what is right.

*Note: To sign this manifesto, or get a copy for your church,
go to wetoo.org/wetoomanifesto.*

THE WE TOO AWARD

If you know of a ministry, missions organization, or church that exemplifies the prophetic imagination from the last chapter, go to wetoo.org/wetooaward and nominate them. Every year, we will recognize those who have fought for the voiceless.

SEXUAL ABUSE RESOURCES

For an updated and constantly revised list of comprehensive sexual abuse resources for individuals, churches, and ministries, visit wetoo.org/resources.

MEDIA INQUIRIES

For all media inquiries, please visit wetoo.org/media to book Mary to speak at your event or book her in media outlets.

WEBSITE

For all other information about *We Too*, please visit wetoo.org.

ACKNOWLEDGMENTS

I wrote this book in a flurry, often heavy hearted, and with painstaking attention to getting it right. To my friend Mick Silva, who graciously shepherded the beginning of this idea, I say a kingdom-laced thank you. To my husband, Patrick, I needed you more in writing this book than with any other project. You prayed. You held. You remained a constant and consistent source of strength for me. I love you. To our church, Lake Pointe, and our Life Group, I appreciate all the love, support, and prayers over the years. I wrote this book, not from a position of animosity toward the church, but with overflowing gratitude for what the church has done and been for me.

How do I possibly thank the sexual abuse recovery community? I'm not really sure how, and I'm afraid I'll miss someone. But thank you, dear Boz Tchividjian. You have been a friend, mentor, and truly a man who exemplifies grace. Jules Woodson, what a story you have, and what a movement that has sparked as you bravely told your story. Jimmy Hinton, you have given me hope that this crazy train can turn around, and it will be because of folks like you who dared to turn in a pedophile—your father. I'm grateful for all who participated in the For Such a Time as This rally, spearheaded beautifully by Cheryl Summers. Thank you Charissa Dvorak, Ashley Easter, Wade Burleson, Mike Sloan, Dee Ann Miller, Beth Hart, David Pittman, Wade Mullen, Ryan Ashton, Christa Brown, Rebecca Davis, Jacob and Rachael Denhollander, Amy Smith, Dee Parsons, and Justin and Lindsey Holcomb for your advocacy. I appreciate the prayers of unnamed friends who have walked their own journeys but would rather not be mentioned. I *so* get that.

Gratitude abounds for the Writing Prayer Circle, who prayed for me for more than 15 years now—all faithful friends. Thank you, Kathi, Sandi, Holly, Renee, Caroline, Cheramy, Jeanne, D'Ann, Darren, Dorian, Erin, Helen, Katy G., Katy R., Anita, Diane, Cyndi, Leslie, Liz, Rebecca, Sarah, Tim, Tina, Nicole, Tosca, TJ, Patrick, Jody, Susan, Becky, Dena, Carol, Susie, Christy, Alice, Randy, Paul, Jan, Thomas, Judy, Aldyth, Sue, Brandilyn, Lisa, Richard, Michele, Yanci, Cristin, Roy, Michelle, Ocieanna, Denise, Heidi, Kristin, Sarah, Phyllis, Emilie,

Lea Ann, Boz, Patricia, Anna, Kendra, Gina, Ralph, Sophie, Anna, Jodie, Hope, Ellen, Lacy, Tracy, Susie May, Becky, Paula, John, Julie, Dusty, Tabea, Jessica, Cheri, Shelley, Elain, Ally, Lilly, Sabina, and Amy.

Thank you to David and Sarah VanDiest, who have not only shepherded my career, but have welcomed me into their home and hearts.

How can I thank you, Harvest House? Bob Hawkins, thank you for taking a risk and for sharing the book with your wife, Beth. Thank you, Kathleen Kerr, for hooking me up with the best bakery in Eugene, followed by the best company alongside. Sherrie Slopianka, I'm humbled (and amused) that you were first a fangirl! Thanks for your zeal for the message of this book. You're the best at commiserating, Jessica Ballestrazze. You understand this business but also have a kingdom perspective. Thanks, Christianne Debysingh, for your connections and public relations genius. I appreciate your heart, Ken Lorenz. You're more than a salesman; you're my friend. Brad Moses, what I love about you is the way you treat people—with warmhearted interest. Kathy Zemper, I will be praying alongside you that this book reaches an international audience. Betty Fletcher, I love your brain! Kyler Dougherty, art director extraordinaire, thank you. You "get" my need for creativity, and the cover so aptly reflects that.

JD, thank you for crafting such a heartfelt foreword to the book. That you read it, absorbed its message, and endeavored to encourage others to do the same is a humbling blessing to me. Thank you for tirelessly standing in the gap for this issue, for pioneering a rocky path. It's heroic.

Sophie, Aidan, and Julia, I wrote this book for you. I want you to step into a more just world, where this infiltrating evil is exposed and dealt with. You are the next generation of warriors, and I pray for you constantly.

Jesus, you are everything to me. Everything. I praise you from the bottom of my lungs with every breath within because you noticed me, empathized with my plight, saved me in every way, and gave me a story to tell. You, as always, get the glory.

NOTES

AS YOU READ THIS BOOK

1. This prayer originated in an e-mail message from Dr. Ralph Chen-Green, November 4, 2018.

FOREWORD

1. Judith Herman, Trauma and Recovery (New York: Basic Books, 1997), 7-8.

DEAR READER

1. The three part series continues to evolve, but the first article is entitled "Abuse of Faith: 20 Years, 700 Victims: Southern Baptist sexual abuse spreads as leaders resist reforms" by Robert Downen, Lise Olsen, and John Tedesco, *Houston Chronicle*, February 10, 2019. https://www.houstonchron icle.com/news/investigations/article/Southern-Baptist-sexual-abuse-spreads-as-leaders-13588038 .php?utm_campaign=chron&utm_source=article&utm_medium=https%3A%2F%2Fwww .chron.com%2Fnews%2Finvestigations%2Farticle%2FInvestigation-reveals-700-victims-of -Southern-13591612.php.

2. I'm indebted to Doug Lay's Facebook post that read: "Jeopardy: The priest and the Levite did not tell anyone about the man bleeding on the side of the road. What is a church cover-up?" https:// www.facebook.com/proflay/posts/582849044832.

3. Letter from Lake Pointe Church, "Continuing to Provide a Safe Place for our Children," dated February 15, 2019 at 5:21 PM. Used by permission.

FIRST—THE EXAM ROOM, THE BACK DOOR, AND THE DANCE FLOOR

1. Josiah Hesse, "Billy Graham's Grandson Says Protestants Abuse Kids Just Like Catholics," VICE, August 24, 2017, www.vice.com/en_us/article/xwwd3w/billy-grahams-grandson-says-protestants -abuse-kids-just-like-catholics.

2. Jimmy Hinton, "Shaun Dougherty Unpacks the PA Grand Jury Report," August 30, 2018, in *The Speaking Out on Sexual Abuse Podcast,* https://jimmyhinton.org/podcast.

3. Amanda Casanova, "University Professor Resigns After Allegations of Inappropriate Sexual Con- duct, Christian Headlines, July 20, 2018, www.christianheadlines.com/blog/university-professor -resigns-after-allegations-of-inappropriate-sexual-conduct.html.

4. Harper Lee, *To Kill a Mockingbird* (New York: Harper Perennial Modern Classics, 2002), 30.

CHAPTER 1—RAPE: THE BIBLICAL CONUNDRUM

1. "Sexual Abuse," American Psychological Association, accessed November 28, 2018, https:// www .apa.org/topics/sexual-abuse/index.aspx.

2. For an extensive list of types of sexual abuse, see the Rape, Abuse & Incest National Network at www.rainn.org/types-sexual-violence.

3. David T. Lamb, "David Was a Rapist, Abraham Was a Sex Trafficker," *Christianity Today*, Octo- ber 22, 2015, www.christianitytoday.com/ct/2015/october-web-only/david-was-rapist-abraham -was-sex-trafficker.html.

4. Ibid.

5. Katie McCoy, "Did Old Testament Law Force a Woman to Marry Her Rapist?" *The Council on Biblical Manhood and Womanhood*, March 5, 2018, cbmw.org/topics/sex/did-old-testament-law-force-a-woman-to-marry-her-rapist.

6. David T. Lamb, "David Was a Rapist, Abraham Was a Sex Trafficker."

7. "Hagar Meaning," Abarim Publications, November 21, 2017, www.abarim-publications.com/Meaning/Hagar.html.

CHAPTER 2—THE REVOLUTIONARY RESPONDER: JESUS

1. Frank Viola and Mary DeMuth, *The Day I Met Jesus* (Grand Rapids, MI: Baker Publishing Group, 2015), 85, 87.

2. Sandra Glahn, "Repentance = Reparations: Time Does Not Heal All Sin," *Bible.org,* November 6, 2018, https//blogs.bible.org/engage/sandra_glahn/repentance_reparations_time_does_not_heal_all_sin.

CHAPTER 3—ABUSE AND THE CHURCH

1. Lloyd deMause, "The History of Child Abuse," *The Journal of Psychohistory* 25, no. 3 (Winter 1998): http://psychohistory.com/articles/the-history-of-child-abuse.

2. Steven Mintz, "Placing Childhood Sexual Abuse in Historical Perspective," *The Immanent Frame*, July 13, 2012, https://tif.ssrc.org/2012/07/13/placing-childhood-sexual-abuse-in-historical-perspective/.

3. Ibid.

4. Ryan Scheel, "How the Ancient Catholic Church Dealt with Priest Sex Offenders," uCatholic, July 24, 2018, https://www.ucatholic.com/blog/how-the-ancient-catholic-church-dealt-with-priest-sex-offenders.

5. Ibid.

6. Patrick J. Wall, "Celibacy, Sex & Catholic Church," *Richard Sipe,* accessed January 28, 2019, http://www.awrsipe.com/patrick_wall/executive_summary.htm.

7. William Lobdell, "Vatican Aware of Abuse for Centuries, Study Says," *Los Angeles Times*, June 20, 2004, http://articles.latimes.com/2004/jun/20/local/me-priests20.

8. Curtis Harris, "The Loathsome Den: Sexual Assault on the Plantation, #MeToo of the 19th Century," *President Lincoln's Cottage*, December 19, 2017, www.lincolncottage.org/the-loathsome-den-sexual-assault-on-the-plantation-metoo.

9. Valerie Tarico, "Conservative Christianity's Marketing Gimmick to Keep Its Old-Time, Heaven-and-Hell Religion Afloat," *Progressive Values*, July 10, 2012, http://progressivevalues.org/conservative-christianitys-marketing-gimmick-to-keep-its-old-time-heaven-and-hell-religion-afloat-by-valerie-tarico.

10. Ibid.

11. Sigal Samuel, "The Sex-Abuse Scandal Is Growing Faster than the Church Can Handle It," *The Atlantic*, September 14, 2018, www.theatlantic.com/international/archive/2018/09/catholic-sex-abuse-pope-francis/570208.

12. Josiah Hesse, "Billy Graham's Grandson Says Protestants Abuse Kids Just Like Catholics," *VICE*, August 24, 2017, www.vice.com/en_us/article/xwwd3w/billy-grahams-grandson-says-protestants-abuse-kids-just-like-catholics.

13. Manya A. Brachear, "Missionary Child Abuse, Long Unspoken of, Emerges from the Shadows,"

Chicago Tribune, June 17, 2013, www.chicagotribune.com/news/ct-xpm-2013-06-17-ct-met
-missionary-abuse-20130617-story.html.

CHAPTER 4—THE POWER OF SECRETS

1. Stoyan Zaimov, "Toby Willis' Daughter Jessica Reveals Decades of Sexual Abuse, Beating, Secrets in Christian Family," *The Christian Post*, April 17, 2018, www.christianpost.com/news/ toby-willis-daughter-jessica-reveals-decades-sex-abuse-beatings-secrets-christian-family-223022.

2. "Fr Finnegan: Survivor Speaks of Sex Abuse 'Secret,'" *BBC News*, February 8, 2018, https://www .bbc.com/news/uk-northern-ireland-42991175.

3. Jana Hollingsworth and Brooks Johnson, "'An Awful Secret': 2 Generations' Struggle to Be Heard About Sexual Abuse," *TwinCities.com Pioneer Press*, April 16, 2018, https://www.twincities .com/2018/04/16/an-awful-secret-2-generations-struggle-to-be-heard-about-sexual-abuse.

4. Megha Mohan, "Secret World: The Women in the UK Who Cannot Report Sexual Abuse," March 27, 2017, www.bbc.com/news/in-pictures-43499374.

5. Meera Senthilingam, "Sexual Harassment: How It Stands Around the Globe," CNN, November 29, 2018, www.cnn.com/2017/11/25/health/sexual-harassment-violence-abuse-global-levels/ index.html.

6. Ibid.

7. W.C. Holmes and G.B. Slap, "Sexual Abuse of Boys: Definition, Prevalence Correlates, Sequelae, and Management," *Journal of the American Medical Association* 280, no. 21 (December 2, 1998): 1855-62, doi:10.1001/jama.280.21.1855.

CHAPTER 5—THE PERSUASIVENESS OF BAD THEOLOGY

1. Rachael Denhollander, "Justice: The Foundation of a Christian Approach to Abuse," *Fathom*, November 19, 2018, https://www.fathommag.com/stories/justice-the-foundation-of-a-christian -approach-to-abuse.

2. Morgan Lee, "My Larry Nassar Testimony Went Viral. But There's More to the Gospel Than Forgiveness," *Christianity Today*, January 31, 2018, https://www.christianitytoday.com/ct/2018/ january-web-only/rachael-denhollander-larry-nassar-forgiveness-gospel.html.

3. Ted Dekker, from a January 28, 2006 blog post on teddekker.com, accessed April 7, 2007.

4. Denhollander, "Justice."

5. Ibid.

6. Ibid.

CHAPTER 6—THE PERVASIVENESS OF PORN

1. Mary DeMuth, *Beautiful Battle* (Eugene, OR: Harvest House Publishers, 2012), 98.

2. Timothy Keller, *Counterfeit Gods* (New York: Penguin, 2009), 165-66.

3. Morgan Lee, "Here's How 770 Pastors Describe Their Struggle with Porn," *Christianity Today*, January 26, 2016, www.christianitytoday.com/news/2016/january/how-pastors-struggle-porn -phenomenon-josh-mcdowell-barna.html.

4. Bo Lane, "How Many Pastors Are Addicted to Porn? The Stats are Surprising," *Expastors*, March 25, 2014, www.expastors.com/how-many-pastors-are-addicted-to-porn-the-stats-are-surprising.

5. Mary DeMuth, *Thin Places: A Memoir* (Grand Rapids, MI: Zondervan, 2010), 125-26.

6. See https://beggarsdaughter.com.

7. Jessica Harris, e-mail message to author, November 20, 2018.

8. "The Facts," *Pornography + Sex Trafficking,* accessed December 29, 2015, http://stoptrafficking demand.com/facts.

9. Alexis Kleinman, "Porn Sites Get More Visitors Each Month Than Netflix, Amazon and Twitter Combined," *Huffington Post,* December 6, 2017, www.huffingtonpost.com/2013/05/03/internet -porn-stats_n_3187682.html.

10. "Internet Pornography by the Numbers; A Significant Threat to Society," Webroot Smarter Cyber-security, accessed January 28, 2019, https://www.webroot.com/us/en/resources/tips-articles/ internet-pornography-by-the-numbers.

11. Visit the Internet Watch Foundation at www.iwf.org.uk for more information.

12. "Know More: Child Pornography Facts," The Innocent Justice Foundation, accessed January 28, 2019, http://innocentjustice.org/know-more.

13. "Internet Pornography by the Numbers; A Significant Threat to Society."

14. Kleinman, "Porn Sites Get More Visitors Each Month Than Netflix, Amazon and Twitter Combined."

15. "Internet Pornography by the Numbers."

16. "Sex Trafficking," Polaris, accessed January 28, 2019, https://polarisproject.org/human-trafficking/ sex-trafficking.

17. "How Porn Fuels Toxic Rape Culture and Sexual Assault on College Campuses," Fight the New Drug, May 2, 2018, https://fightthenewdrug.org/how-porn-is-fueling-sexual-assault-on-college -campuses/.

18. Ibid.

19. "Is There a Connection Between Porn Culture and Rape Culture?" Fight the New Drug, September 19, 2017, https://fightthenewdrug.org/violence-and-rape-connected-with-porn.

20. "Pornography and Public Health: Research Summary," National Center on Sexual Exploita-tion, September 8, 2016, https://endsexualexploitation.org/wp-content/uploads/NCOSE_ PornographyPH_RESEARCH-SUMMARY_9-8-16.pdf.

21. "Is There a Connection Between Porn Culture and Rape Culture?"

22. Ibid.

23. Robert Jensen, "Pornography and Sexual Violence," National Online Resource Center on Vio-lence Against Women, July 2004, http://vawnet.org/sites/default/files/materials/files/2016-09/ AR_PornAndSV.pdf.

24. Jessica Harris, e-mail message to author, November 20, 2018.

25. DeMuth, *Beautiful Battle,* 97.

CHAPTER 7—THE PROBLEM OF PREDATORS

1. Kerry Howley, "Everyone Believed Larry Nassar," *The Cut,* November 19, 2018, www.thecut .com/2018/11/how-did-larry-nassar-deceive-so-many-for-so-long.html.

2. Mary DeMuth, *The Seven Deadly Friendships* (Eugene, OR: Harvest House Publishers, 2018), 67-68.

3. Mary DeMuth, "13 Surprising Traits of Predatory People That You Might Just Overlook," *FaithIt,* December 29, 2016, https://faithit.com/13-signs-predatory-people-mary-demuth/.

4. Judy D.J. Ellich, "Pastor Trying to Deal with the Sins of His Father," *Daily American*, November 19, 2018, https://www.dailyamerican.com/news/local/somerset/pastor-trying-to-deal-with-the -sins-of-his-father/article_cbbd6654-c5f2-55f9-9210-41bbc757403e.html.

5. Laurie Goodstein, "Church Abuse Report Authors Defend Findings as Critics Weigh In," *The New York Times*, May 18, 2011, https://www.nytimes.com/2011/05/19/us/19bishops.html. To read the entire report, visit http://www.usccb.org/issues-and-action/child-and-youth-protection/ upload/The-Causes-and-Context-of-Sexual-Abuse-of-Minors-by-Catholic-Priests-in-the -United-States-1950-2010.pdf.

6. "Myths and Facts About Sex Offenders," Center for Sex Offender Management, August 2000, https://ccoso.org/sites/default/files/import/mythsfacts.pdf.

7. Mary DeMuth, "Be Wise About Repentant Predators," MaryDeMuth.com, September 16, 2018, https://www.marydemuth.com/repentant-predators.

8. My thoughts are influenced by Boz Tchividjian in "Where Are the Voices?" GRACE, November 11, 2018, https://www.netgrace.org/resources/2018/11/11/where-are-the-voices.

9. Jimmy Hinton, conversation with author, November 2018.

CHAPTER 8—THE PASSIVITY OF THE CHURCH

1. Rachael Denhollander, "Justice: The Foundation of a Christian Approach to Abuse," *Fathom*, November 19, 2018, https://www.fathommag.com/stories/justice-the-foundation-of-a-christian -approach-to-abuse.

2. Brett Sengstock, interviewed in "Victim of Hillsong Church Founder's Father Says Childhood Was Destroyed by Sexual Abuse," 60 Minutes Australia, November 19, 2018, https://www.youtube .com/watch?v=4g2FgAu1NYw.

3. Ibid.

4. "Fr Finnegan: Survivor Speaks of Sex Abuse 'Secret,'" *BBC News*, February 8, 2018, https://www .bbc.com/news/uk-northern-ireland-42991175.

5. Sarah Smith, "Southern Baptist Officials Knew of Sexual Abuse Allegations 11 Years Before Leader's Arrest," *Fort Worth Star Telegram*, July 13, 2018, https://www.star-telegram.com/living/ religion/article214758515.html.

6. Megan Briggs, "SBC Apologizes to Sexual Abuse Victim Anne Miller," *Church Leaders*, July 26, 2018, https://churchleaders.com/news/329633-sbc-apologizes-sexual-abuse-victim-anne-miller .html.

7. Brendan Cole, "3,677 Sexual Abuse Cases in German Catholic Church Reported, with Half the Victims Under 13," *Newsweek*, September 12, 2018, www.newsweek.com/more-3600-sexual -abuse-cases-german-catholic-church-half-victims-were-under-1117946.

8. Euan McKirdy, "French Bishops Launch 'Independent' Commission on Sex Abuse in Catholic Church," CNN, November 8, 2018, https://edition.cnn.com/2018/11/08/europe/french-bishops -sexual-abuse-commission-intl/index.html.

9. Czarina Ong, "Mennonites Confront Their Church's History of Sexual Abuse, Offers Apologies to Victims," *Christian Today*, July 9, 2015, www.christiantoday.com/article/mennonites-confront -their-churchs-history-of-sexual-abuse-offer-apologies-to-victims/58375.htm.

10. Bob Allen, "Evangelicals 'Worse' than Catholics on Sexual Abuse," *The Christian Century*, October 10, 2013, www.christiancentury.org/article/2013-10/evangelicals-worse-catholics-sexual-abuse.

11. Kate Shellnutt, "Paige Patterson Fired by Southwestern, Stripped of Retirement Benefits," *Chris-*

tianity Today, May 30, 2018, https://www.christianitytoday.com/news/2018/may/paige-patterson
-fired-southwestern-baptist-seminary-sbc.html.

12. Mike Huckabee, "Janet and I want to affirm our support for the Duggar family," Facebook,
    May 22, 2015, https://www.facebook.com/mikehuckabee/posts/janet-and-i-want-to-affirm-our
    -support-for-the-duggar-family-joshs-actions-when-/10152994543137869.

13. Joyce Seelen, quoted in Jim Yardley's article "Abuse by Clergy Is Not Just a Catholic Problem," *The
    New York Times*, April 13, 2002, www.nytimes.com/2002/04/13/us/abuse-by-clergy-is-not-just
    -a-catholic-problem.html.

14. NCR Editorial Staff, "Open Letter to the US Catholic Bishops: It's Over," *National Catholic Reporter*,
    November 9, 2018, www.ncronline.org/news/opinion/open-letter-us-catholic-bishops-its-over.

15. *Paterno*, directed by Barry Levinson (2018, HBO).

16. Mark W. Sanchez, "Paterno Silenced Sandusky Victim in Brutal 1971 Phone Call: Report," *New
    York Post*, May 6, 2016, https://nypost.com/2016/05/06/paterno-silenced-sandusky-victim
    -in-brutal-1971-phone-call-report.

17. I owe this concept to victim advocate David Pittman. The original quotation, from a GBI investi-
    gator, was this: "A pedophile is like a serial killer that leaves his victims alive." See "Pedophiles are
    like Serial Killers—My Story," *Together We Heal*, October 1, 2012, https://togetherweheal.word
    press.com/2012/10/01/pedophiles-are-like-serial-killers-my-story-by-david-pittman.

CHAPTER 9—A NECESSARY EDUCATION

1. "Functional Neurologic Disorders/Conversion Disorder," Mayo Clinic, July 11, 2017, www.mayo
   clinic.org/diseases-conditions/conversion-disorder/symptoms-causes/syc-20355197.

2. This account is quoted in Mary Dickson's article, "A Woman's Worst Nightmare," PBS, 1996,
   https://www.pbs.org/kued/nosafeplace/articles/nightmare.html.

3. N.T. Wright, *Evil and the Justice of God* (Downers Grove, IL: IVP, 2006), 89.

4. Mary DeMuth, "In a Duggar World, the Real Victims Take a Back Seat to Their Parents," *The
   Washington Post*, June 5, 2015, www.washingtonpost.com/news/acts-of-faith/wp/2015/06/05/
   in-a-duggar-world-the-real-victims-take-a-back-seat-to-their-parents.

5. Ibid.

6. Ibid.

7. I will not dignify this person by naming names.

8. Mary DeMuth, "In Faith Communities Like the Duggars, Abuse Victims Are Encouraged to Be
   Filled with Grace. It's Not That Simple," *The Washington Post*, May 22, 2015, www.washington
   post.com/news/acts-of-faith/wp/2015/05/22/why-we-cant-expect-sex-abuse-victims-to
   -generate-instant-forgiveness/?utm_term=.3b4361697da7.

9. Kyle Stephens, "The Basement," November 5, 2018, in the *Believed* podcast, www.npr.org/2018/
   11/01/663152331/the-basement. This episode may be triggering to survivors.

10. Jimmy Hinton (@jimmyhinton12), Twitter, November 27, 2018, 11:13 a.m., https://twitter.com/
    JimmyHinton12/status/1067466476523798528.

11. Her responses and discourse can be found on this post: https://www.facebook.com/photo.php?
    fbid=10155492267341300.

CHAPTER 10—A NUANCED CULTURAL SHIFT FROM HOW-TO TO #METOO

1. Mariyam Saigal, "11 Heart-Wrenching Quotes On #MeToo That'll Make You Cry," *Medium*,

October 31 2017, https://stories.yourquote.in/10-heart-wrenching-quotes-on-metoo-thatll -make-you-cry-af984f889300.

2. Richard Rohr, *Everything Belongs: The Gift of Contemplative Prayer* (New York: The Crossroad Publishing Company, 1999), 144.

3. James Clear, "Why Facts Don't Change Our Minds," blog post, accessed January 28, 2019, https:// jamesclear.com/why-facts-dont-change-minds.

4. Ibid.

CHAPTER 11—A NEW PATHWAY FORWARD

1. Diane Langberg, quoted in Phil Monroe's article, "Must Read: Diane Langberg on 'Trauma as a Mission Field,'" Musings of a Christian Psychologist, June 20, 2011, https://philipmonroe .com/2011/06/20/must-read-diane-langberg-on-trauma-as-a-mission-field.

2. Sarah Mullally, "Ad Clerum from Bishop Sarah—Promoting a Safer Diocese," e-mail message, November 8, 2018, http://newsletters.london.anglican.org/linkapp/cmaview.aspx?LinkID=pageid 100407850qjt-f-njqjf-nfxjjx-z-x-f-f-n.

3. "'Believed' Podcast Tells the Story of Survivors Who Won Justice Against Larry Nassar," NPR, October 15, 2018, www.npr.org/about-npr/656853471/believed-tells-the-story-of-survivors-who-won -justice-against-larry-nassar.

4. For the remainder of this chapter, these people gave permission to use their first name and statements for this book—a request I made on Facebook and Twitter in November of 2018.

5. D. Lisak, L. Garinier, S.C. Nicksa, and A.M. Cote, "False Allegations of Sexual Assault: An Analysis of Ten Years of Reported Cases," *Violence Against Women* 16, no. 12 (December 2010): 1318-34, doi:10.1177/1077801210387747.

6. Heather Davediuk Gingrich, "How to Become a Trauma-Informed Congregation," *Christianity Today*, accessed November 28, 2018, www.christianitytoday.com/pastors/2018/fall-state-of -church-ministry/how-to-become-trauma-informed-congregation.html.

7. A good introductory book for children is *God Made All of Me: A Book to Help Children Protect Their Bodies,* by Justin and Lindsey Holcomb (Greensboro, NC: New Growth Press, 2018).

8. Boz Tchividjian, "The Imbalance & Exploitation of Power: A Recipe for Abuse" Covenant College, November 16, 2018, www.netgrace.org/resources/a-recipe-for-abuse.

9. Joshua Pease, "How the Church Messed Up—And Can Redeem—Its #MeToo Moment," *Relevant*, accessed January 28, 2019, https://relevantmagazine.com/issues/issue-96/itstime.

10. Robert Cunningham, "Addressing Our Past," Tates Creek Presbyterian Church, June 24, 2018, https://tcpca.org/addressing-our-past.

11. Ibid.

12. Ibid.

13. Pease, "How the Church Messed Up—And Can Redeem—Its #MeToo Moment."

14. Facebook interaction with the author, November 2017.

15. Jimmy Hinton, "Convicted Sexual Predator Pastor at Fellowship Bible Church: I've Been Forgiven," JimmyHinton.com, November 9, 2018, http://jimmyhinton.org/convicted-sexual -predator-pastor-at-fellowship-bible-church-ive-been-forgiven.

16. Ibid.

17. See what they provide here: https://www.netgrace.org/independent-investigations.

18. Pease, "How the Church Messed Up—And Can Redeem—Its #MeToo Moment."

19. "Protect your faith community," GRACE, https://www.netgrace.org/safeguarding-certification.

20. Here are two registries to check: www.nationalalertregistry.com and www.nsopw.gov/Core/Portal.aspx.

21. Basyle Tchividjian and Shira M. Berkovits, *The Child Safeguarding Policy Guide for Churches and Ministries* (Greensboro, NC: New Growth Press 2017), 64.

22. Here's an example of how the United Methodist Church approaches it: "Church Participation by a Registered Child Sex Offender," accessed January 28, 2019, www.umc.org/what-we-believe/church-participation-by-a-registered-child-sex-offender.

23. I'm indebted to Angel Ricchuiti and her extensive e-mail about this subject dated November 18, 2018.

24. Tchividjian, "The Imbalance & Exploitation of Power."

25. Jeff Haanen, "Cover Story: God of the Second Shift," *Christianity Today*, September 20, 2018, www.christianitytoday.com/ct/2018/october/theology-of-work-god-of-second-shift.html.

26. Chuck Roberts, Facebook message, November 2017.

27. Megan Briggs, "Beth Moore Leans on Tenure to Call Out Sexism in the Church," *Church Leaders,* November 26, 2018, https://churchleaders.com/news/338187-beth-moore-leans-on-tenure-to-call-out-sexism-in-the-church.html.

28. Jules Woodson, e-mail message to author, November 28, 2018.

29. Drew Dyck, "How Can You Shepherd a Flock You Don't Know?" *Christianity Today*, December 2018, 74.

CHAPTER 12—A PROPHETIC IMAGINATION

1. Robert Cunningham, "Addressing Our Past," Tates Creek Presbyterian Church, June 24, 2018, https://tcpca.org/addressing-our-past.

2. "'Drop by Drop': How Poetry Helped the Military in Afghanistan," WOSU Public Media, July 16, 2018, http://radio.wosu.org/post/drop-drop-how-poetry-helped-us-military-afghanistan #stream /0.

3. N.T. Wright, *Evil and the Justice of God* (Downers Grove, IL: IVP Books 2006), 118.

More from Mary DeMuth

HEALING EVERY DAY

Whatever your circumstance, *Healing Every Day* asks only that you come right where you are to begin a 90-day journey of restoration through the Bible to a healthier, more whole you. As you read Scripture from Genesis to Revelation and allow these devotions to penetrate your heart, you will gain new insights into your past trauma and your hoped-for relief for your present and future joy.

Every day as you say yes to Mary's question *Mind if I pray for you*, you will discover the God who loves you fiercely—right now. He longs to heal your hurting soul. He loves you. He is *for* you. And He's waiting to meet you in all your broken places.

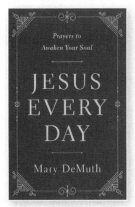

JESUS EVERY DAY

Trying to juggle all your worries and burdens alone? As the challenges of everyday life threaten to continually distract you, your conversations with God can start to feel threadbare—too rushed to touch on the real issues that crowd your heart.

Rediscover your compassionate Savior with this collection of daily heart-provoking prayers and accompanying Scriptures. Each reading will awaken your tired soul, prompt new ways to encounter Jesus, and inaugurate the kind of authentic conversation you've always yearned to have with Him.

To learn more about Harvest House books and
to read sample chapters, visit our website:

www.harvesthousepublishers.com

HARVEST HOUSE PUBLISHERS
EUGENE, OREGON